8/25/13

Dear Jen,

A friend gave me this book many years ago and it has helped guide me in my walk with Jesus! You are a beautiful person with a sincere, caring heart and I have loved getting to know you! Stay close to Jesus and His Word in all you do!

Congratulations on your baptism today!

Love in Christ,

Jennalee

# 90 Days with the
# CHRISTIAN
# CLASSICS

## ONE MINUTE BIBLE

# 90 Days with the CHRISTIAN CLASSICS

## ONE MINUTE BIBLE

*Devotions From Yesterday... For Today*

*Contributing Editors:*

## MICHAEL BAUMAN, LAWRENCE KIMBROUGH, MARTIN I. KLAUBER, KEITH P. WELLS

HOLMAN
REFERENCE

Nashville, Tennessee

One Minute Bible–*90 Days with the Christian Classics*
Copyright © 1999 Broadman & Holman Publishers
Nashville, Tennessee, 37234
All rights reserved

ISBN 0-8054-9278-X

Dewey Decimal Classification: 242.
Subject Heading: Bible: Meditations
Library of Congress Card Catalog Number: 99–15733

Production Staff
*Executive Editor:* David Shepherd
*Editor:* Lawrence Kimbrough
*Project Editor:* Lloyd Mullens
*Design Team:* Wendell Overstreet, Anderson Thomas Graphics
*Typesetting:* TF Designs
*Production:* Kevin Kunce

**Library of Congress Cataloging-in-Publication Data**
Kimbrough, Lawrence, 1963–
   One minute Bible: ninety days with the Christian Classics / Lawrence Kimbrough,
     author/compiler; Michael Bauman . . . [et al.], contributing editors.
       p. cm.
   Includes bibliographical references.
   ISBN 0-8054-9278-X
   1. Devotional calendars. I. Bauman, Michael. II. Title.
BV4810.K54   1999
242'.2–dc21                                  99–15733
                                                          CIP

Printed in United States of America
2 3 4 5 6 03 02
[Q]

# Contents

# TO SEE YOUR FACE

THE SCRIPTURE SAYS THAT NO ONE HAS EVER SEEN GOD AND LIVED TO TELL ABOUT IT. YET STRANGELY, WE LONG TO DRAW NEARER THE FIRE—RISKING LIFE AS WE KNOW IT, IF ONLY THE BLAZING GLORY OF GOD WILL MELT AWAY EVERYTHING THAT'S IMPURE ABOUT US AND WE CAN DISCOVER ALL THAT REALLY MATTERS IN LIFE IN THE FIRST PLACE . . . IN HIS EYES.

## Psalm 63:1-8; 84:1-2

*O God, you are my God, earnestly I seek you; my soul thirsts for you, my body longs for you, in a dry and weary land where there is no water.*

*I have seen you in the sanctuary and beheld your power and your glory. Because your love is better than life, my lips will glorify you.*

*I will praise you as long as I live, and in your name I will lift up my hands. My soul will be satisfied as with the richest of foods; with singing lips my mouth will praise you.*

*On my bed I remember you; I think of you through the watches of the night. Because you are my help, I sing in the shadow of your wings. My soul clings to you; your right hand upholds me. . .*

*How lovely is your dwelling place, O LORD Almighty! My soul yearns, even faints, for the courts of the LORD; my heart and my flesh cry out for the living God.*

PERSONALLY SPEAKING *Drawing near to God means drawing away from other things–empty-calorie pursuits that can taste pretty good but never satisfy. Push away from the table today. And enjoy His company.*

My Lord and my Creator,
you bear with me and nourish me–be my helper.
I thirst for you, I hunger for you, I desire you,
    I sigh for you, I covet you:
I am like an orphan deprived of the presence
    of a very kind father,
who, weeping and wailing, does not cease to cling to
    the dear face with his whole heart.
So, as much as I can, though not as much as I ought,
    I am mindful of your passion,
your buffeting, your scourging, your
cross, your wounds,
    how you were slain for me, how pre-
pared for burial and buried;
and also I remember your glorious
resurrection,
    and wonderful ascension.
All this I hold with unwavering faith,
    and weep over the hardship of exile,
hoping in the sole consolation of your
coming, ardently longing for the glorious
contemplation of your face.
–Anselm

ANSELM OF
CANTERBURY
(1033-1109)

As archbishop of
Canterbury, Anselm
was exiled twice by
English kings for
insisting on church
reform, but
returned in 1107 to
continue his push
for clerical purity. A
gifted teacher and
thinker, many of his
writings are dia-
logues with stu-
dents, answering
the honest ques-
tions of youth.
Believing that faith
was the foundation
of all spiritual pur-
suit, he wrote, "I do
not seek to under-
stand that I may
believe, but I
believe that I may
understand: for this
also I believe, that
unless I believe, I
will not
understand."

# The Best Is Yet to Come

Life is a little like Christmas morning. With each camera flash and new paper wad, the pile of presents gets smaller, another fifteen minutes slip away, and you catch yourself torn between enjoying the moment and missing the part that's already gone. It's happy, but it's sad. But life won't be like that forever. One great, big, glorious day, there will be no end to God's presence.

## Romans 8:18-25

*I consider that our present sufferings are not worth comparing with the glory that will be revealed in us.*

*The creation waits in eager expectation for the sons of God to be revealed. For the creation was subjected to frustration, not by its own choice, but by the will of the one who subjected it, in hope that the creation itself will be liberated from its bondage to decay and brought into the glorious freedom of the children of God.*

*We know that the whole creation has been groaning as in the pains of childbirth right up to the present time. Not only so, but we ourselves, who have the firstfruits of the Spirit, groan inwardly as we wait eagerly for our adoption as sons, the redemption of our bodies. For in this hope we were saved.*

*But hope that is seen is no hope at all. Who hopes for what he already has? But if we hope for what we do not yet have, we wait for it patiently.*

PERSONALLY SPEAKING *Happiness and misery will always flow in and out of your life. Whatever stream you find yourself in today, thank God that He's saving something much better for last.*

It seems that man can attain Happiness by his natural powers ... for man is naturally the principle of his action by his intellect and will. But final Happiness prepared for the saints surpasses the intellect and will of man. ...

A certain participation of Happiness can be had in this life, but perfect and true Happiness cannot be had in this life. For since happiness is a perfect and sufficient good, it excludes every evil, and fulfills every desire. But in this life every evil cannot be excluded. For this present life is subject to many unavoidable evils: to ignorance on the part of the intellect, to disordered affection on the part of the appetite, and to many penalties on the part of the body.

Likewise, neither can the desire for good be satisfied in this life. For man naturally desires the good which he has to be abiding. Now the goods of the present life pass away, since life itself passes away, which we naturally desire to have, and would wish to hold abidingly, for man naturally shrinks from death. Therefore, it is impossible to have true Happiness in this life. ...

Imperfect happiness that can be had in this life can be acquired by man by his natural powers ... but man's perfect happiness consists in the vision of [God], the Divine Essence. ... Man is made happy by God alone, if we speak of perfect Happiness.
–Thomas Aquinas

THOMAS AQUINAS (1224-1274)

He endures as perhaps the greatest philosopher and theologian of the medieval church, and his many writings (including the mammoth *Summa Theologica*) continue to influence believers today. Much of his work deals with how little man knows and understands God, since He is a unique, transcendent being, known only by analogy or by what He is not. He also maintained a distinction between moral theology and general ethics, one being divinely revealed and the other naturally accessible to all people.

# LOST AND FOUND

WE'LL NEVER FIGURE THIS ONE OUT THIS SIDE OF FOREVER. THERE'S NO EARTHLY EXPLANATION FOR WHY GOD WOULD OPEN HIMSELF UP TO SUCH TOTAL REJECTION BY HIS CREATION, AND YET WOO THEM WITH A LOVE USUALLY RESERVED FOR THOSE INCLINED TO RETURN THE AFFECTION. THE GOD WHO SEEKS IS ONE OF THE GREATEST MYSTERIES OF LIFE, AND THE PEOPLE WHO TURN FIND THE GOAL OF ALL THEIR SEEKING.

## *Ezekiel 34:11–16a*

"For this is what the Sovereign Lord says: I myself will search for my sheep and look after them. As a shepherd looks after his scattered flock when he is with them, so will I look after my sheep. I will rescue them from all the places where they were scattered on a day of clouds and darkness.

"I will bring them out from the nations and gather them from the countries, and I will bring them into their own land. I will pasture them on the mountains of Israel, in the ravines and in all the settlements in the land. I will tend them in a good pasture, and the mountain heights of Israel will be their grazing land. There they will lie down in good grazing land, and there they will feed in a rich pasture on the mountains of Israel.

"I myself will tend my sheep and make them lie down, declares the Sovereign LORD. I will search for the lost and bring back the strays. I will bind up the injured and strengthen the weak. . . ."

PERSONALLY SPEAKING *We don't really even know yet all the things our salvation has saved us from. Thank God today for the ones He brings to your mind. And for the ones you're yet to see.*

_____

_____

_____

_____

_____

_____

Where then did I find You, that I might learn You? For you were not in my memory before I learned You. Where then did I find You, that I might learn You, but in You above me? Place there is none; we go backward and forward, and there is no place. Every where, O Truth, You give audience to all who ask counsel of You, and at once You answer all, though they ask your counsel on manifold matters. Clearly You do answer, though all do not clearly hear. All consult You on what they will, though they hear not always what they will. He is Your best servant who looks not so much to hear from You that which he wills, as that which he hears from you.

Too late have I loved You, O Beauty of ancient days, yet ever new! Too late have I loved You! And behold, You were within, and I abroad, and there I searched for You; deformed I, plunging amid those fair forms which You have made. You were with me, but I was not with You. Things held me far from You, which, unless they were in You, were not at all. You called, and shouted, and burst my deafness. You flashed, shone, and scattered my blindness. You breathed, and I drew in my breath and panted for You. I tasted, and hungered and thirsted. You touched me, and I burned for Your peace.

–Augustine

AUGUSTINE OF HIPPO (354-430)

The greatest of the Latin fathers, he is best known today for *The Confessions,* which painfully describe his regret for allowing pleasure and ambition to lure him away from Christian faith, as well as The *City of God,* which he wrote in response to the allegation that Christianity was responsible for the sack of Rome in 410. He sought to explain how the kingdoms of the world and the kingdom of God clash by nature over love and loyalty, and why ruin is the inevitable destiny of those who reject God's authority.

# THE FACES OF FRIENDSHIP

THE TELEPHONE BILL. THE WATER BILL. A GROCERY STORE CIRCULAR AND ANOTHER CREDIT CARD APPLICATION. (WONDER WHEN THEY'LL GET THE HINT.) HEY, WAIT! A HANDWRITTEN LETTER, WITH A LIVE STAMP THAT SOMEONE ACTUALLY LICKED AND POUNDED DOWN WITH THEIR OWN FIST. WHICH ONE WOULD YOU OPEN FIRST? HOW DEAR ARE THE WORDS AND THE HEART, THE TIME AND THE TREASURE OF A TRUE FRIEND?

## 1 Samuel 19:1-4a, 5-7

*Saul told his son Jonathan and all the attendants to kill David. But Jonathan was very fond of David and warned him, "My father Saul is looking for a chance to kill you. Be on your guard tomorrow morning; go into hiding and stay there. I will go out and stand with my father in the field where you are. I'll speak to him about you and will tell you what I find out."*

*Jonathan spoke well of David to Saul his father and said to him, "Let not the king do wrong to his servant David . . . He took his life in his hands when he killed the Philistine. The Lord won a great victory for all Israel, and you saw it and were glad. Why then would you do wrong to an innocent man like David by killing him for no reason?"*

*Saul listened to Jonathan and took this oath: "As surely as the LORD lives, David will not be put to death."*

*So Jonathan called David and told him the whole conversation. He brought him to Saul, and David was with Saul as before.*

PERSONALLY SPEAKING *Yes, you're busy. Who's not these days? But surely there's one person, one friend, one quick phone call you can make that would make someone's day. What are friends for?*

_____

_____

_____

_____

_____

_____

Little do men perceive what solitude is, and how far it extendeth. For a crowd is not company; and faces are but a gallery of pictures; and talk but a tinkling cymbal, where there is no love. The Latin adage meeteth with it a little: "A great town is a great solitude," because in a great town friends are scattered; so that there is not that fellowship, for the most part, which is in less neighborhoods. But we may go further, and affirm most truly that it is a mere and miserable solitude to want true friends, without which the world is but a wilderness; and even in this sense also of solitude, whosoever in the frame of his nature and affections is unfit for friendship, he taketh it of the beast, and not from humanity.

A principal fruit of friendship is the ease and discharge of the fulness and swellings of the heart, which passions of all kinds do cause and induce. We know diseases of stoppings and suffocations are the most dangerous in the body, and it is not much otherwise in the mind. You may take sarza to open the liver, steel to open the spleen, flowers of sulphur for the lungs, castoreum for the brain; but no receipt openeth the heart, but a true friend, to whom you may impart griefs, joys, fears, hopes, suspicions, counsels, and whatsoever lieth upon the heart to oppress it.

–Sir Francis Bacon

FRANCIS BACON
(1561-1626)

From a seat in the House of Commons at age 23 to an appointment as lord chancellor for life under James I, Bacon's steady rise in the English government ended when he was charged with accepting a bribe in 1621. He was sentenced to jail and a fine of £40,000, but served only a few days and had his money returned. He spent his remaining years writing books on the advancement of science. He wrote little on religion, but was known as a Christian, despite certain evidence of his being a man of the world.

# FATHER, FORGIVE ME

SURPRISINGLY, THE ROAD TO REAL SELF-ESTEEM COMES THROUGH NEVER ESTEEMING OURSELVES TOO HIGHLY, FROM REALIZING ON A REGULAR BASIS THAT THE VEIL OF OUR OWN HOLINESS IS DANGEROUSLY THIN. AND THAT IF IT WEREN'T FOR A FEW BLOOD-STAINED NAILS HOLDING US IN PLACE, WE'D BE IN NO BETTER ETERNAL SHAPE THAN THE WORST THE WORLD HAS TO OFFER. PEOPLE ON THEIR KNEES KNOW WHERE THEY STAND.

### Psalm 51:17; 1 John 1:8-9; Micah 7:18; James 4:7-10

*The sacrifices of God are a broken spirit; a broken and contrite heart, O God, you will not despise. . . .*

*If we claim to be without sin, we deceive ourselves and the truth is not in us. If we confess our sins, he is faithful and just and will forgive us our sins and purify us from all unrighteousness. . . .*

*Who is a God like you, who pardons sin and forgives the transgression of the remnant of his inheritance? You do not stay angry forever but delight to show mercy. . . .*

*Submit yourselves, then, to God. Resist the devil, and he will flee from you.*

*Come near to God and he will come near to you. Wash your hands, you sinners, and purify your hearts, you double-minded. Grieve, mourn and wail. Change your laughter to mourning and your joy to gloom.*

*Humble yourselves before the Lord, and he will lift you up.*

PERSONALLY SPEAKING *Maybe this would be a good day to break down and straighten your spiritual closets, sweep out from under the bed, gather up your dirty laundry, and remember Whose house you're living in.*

_____

_____

_____

_____

_____

_____

O Father in heaven, who fashioned my limbs to serve You and my soul to follow hard after You, with sorrow and contrition of heart I acknowledge before You the faults and failures of the day.

Too long, O Father, have I tried Your patience; too often have I betrayed the sacred trust You have given me to keep; yet You are still willing that I should come to You in lowliness of heart, as now I do, beseeching You to drown my transgressions in the sea of Your own infinite love.

My failure to be true even to my own accepted standards, my self-deception in face of temptation, my choosing of the worse when I know the better . . .

O Lord forgive.

My failure to apply to myself the standards of conduct I demand of others, my blindness to the suffering of others and my slowness to be taught by my own, my complacence toward wrongs that do not touch my own case and my over-sensitiveness to those that do, my slowness to see the good in my fellows and to see the evil in myself, my hardness of heart toward my neighbor's faults and my readiness to make allowance for my own, my unwillingness to believe that You have called me to a small work and my brother to a great one . . .

O Lord forgive.

–John Baillie

JOHN BAILLIE
(1886-1960)

This Scottish theologian was professor of divinity at the University of Edinburgh. He was even chaplain to the queen in Scotland and was appointed by the church during World War II to convene a commission "for the interpretation of God's will in the present crisis." He excelled as an apologist, deeply concerned with the doubts people felt about the Christian faith, and his *Diary of Private Prayer* reveals a man of grave humility and holiness.

# A Separate Sanctuary

THERE SHOULD ALWAYS BE A PLACE FOR SEEKERS IN THE CHURCH, AS LONG AS WHAT THEY FIND INSIDE IS NOT MERELY A REPACKAGED SERVING OF THE WORLD THEY LIVE IN, BUT A THRIVING GROUP OF BELIEVERS WHO RUN COUNTER TO THE PREVAILING WINDS, WHO ATTRACT NOT MERELY WITH BLUE JEANS AND A RHYTHM SECTION, BUT WITH A MESSAGE AND A GENUINE LOVE THAT MARCH TO A DIFFERENT DRUMMER.

## 1 Peter 2:4-5, 9-12

*As you come to him, the living Stone—rejected by men but chosen by God and precious to him—you also, like living stones, are being built into a spiritual house to be a holy priesthood, offering spiritual sacrifices acceptable to God through Jesus Christ. . . .*

*But you are a chosen people, a royal priesthood, a holy nation, a people belonging to God, that you may declare the praises of him who called you out of darkness into his wonderful light.*

*Once you were not a people, but now you are the people of God; once you had not received mercy, but now you have received mercy.*

*Dear friends, I urge you, as aliens and strangers in the world, to abstain from sinful desires, which war against your soul. Live such good lives among the pagans that, though they accuse you of doing wrong, they may see your good deeds and glorify God on the day he visits us.*

PERSONALLY SPEAKING *Make sure that inviting people to come as they are doesn't mean making them comfortable staying like they've been. Be willing to be different, to discuss, to disciple, to call them a little higher.*

The Church exists in that it becomes visible to the world (whether understood by the world or not) as a living community, living in the sense that it hears and responds to God's Word, stands and delivers as the fellowship of the Holy Spirit . . . It is a question of the event in which this community, in the midst of the world, distinguishes itself from the world and thereby inevitably becomes offensive to the world in a particularly way. It is a question of this community opening wide its doors and windows in order to truly share not in the fraud and especially not in the religious and moralistic illusions of its environment, but in its real concerns, needs, and tasks, that it may present a calm center of lodging and reflection in contrast to the world's activity and idleness, and also in order to be, in this context, the source of prophetic unrest, admonition, and instigation, without which this transitory world can never endure.

And before all else, this community must be open to the world in order to make visible, with its proclamation of the kingdom of God, the clear, but also severe limits of all human movement and effort, progress and regress, ascents and descents. The Church does not exist by pondering, studying, discussing, and preparing itself for this relationship to the world. The Church exists in actually accomplishing this relationship in each time with the appropriate sense of security, realism, and necessity.

–Karl Barth

KARL BARTH
(1886-1968)

He taught at several of Germany's leading universities before returning to his native Switzerland as the Nazis ascended to power. In all, he wrote over 500 books, articles, and papers, including an unfinished thirteen-book set entitled *Church Dogmatics*. His theology included an emphasis on the Bible as being God's sole revelation of His Word, which he amplified to include the revelation that came through Jesus, the Incarnate Word, and surmised that man can only be understood by seeing him as he is in Christ.

# SAFE IN YOUR ARMS

IMAGINE A WORLD WHERE DOORKNOBS DON'T RATTLE IN THE NIGHT, WHERE VIDEO STORES CARRY THINGS YOUR FAMILY CAN ACTUALLY WATCH, WHERE CHURCH NURSERIES DON'T REQUIRE SECURITY POLICIES AND BACKGROUND CHECKS. THERE AREN'T MANY SAFE PLACES IN OUR WORLD ANYMORE. BUT THERE'S A PLACE WHERE GOD'S PROMISED TO KEEP US SAFE FOREVER. AND THE DEVIL HIMSELF CAN'T DO ANYTHING TO STOP IT.

## Romans 8:33–39

*Who will bring any charge against those whom God has chosen? It is God who justifies.*

*Who is he that condemns? Christ Jesus, who died–more than that, who was raised to life–is at the right hand of God and is also interceding for us.*

*Who shall separate us from the love of Christ? Shall trouble or hardship or persecution or famine or nakedness or danger or sword? As it is written: "For your sake we face death all day long; we are considered as sheep to be slaughtered."*

*No, in all these things we are more than conquerors through him who loved us.*

*For I am convinced that neither death nor life, neither angels nor demons, neither the present nor the future, nor any powers, neither height nor depth, nor anything else in all creation, will be able to separate us from the love of God that is in Christ Jesus our Lord.*

PERSONALLY SPEAKING *There's a safe place in your future, where the past can no longer haunt and the pressure can no longer get to you. Lie down and rest today. You'll never be out of God's love. How's that for some good news?*

Christian, believe this, and think on it: you shall be eternally embraced in the arms of that love which was from everlasting, and will extend to everlasting; of that love which brought the Son of God's love from heaven to earth, from earth to the cross, from the cross to the grave, from the grave to glory; that love which was weary, hungry, tempted, scorned, scourged, buffeted, spit upon, crucified, pierced; which did fast, pray, teach, heal, weep, sweat, bleed, die; that love will eternally embrace thee.

When perfect created love and most perfect uncreated love meet together, it will not be like Joseph and his brethren, who lay upon one another's necks weeping; it will be loving and rejoicing, not loving and sorrowing. Yes, it will make Satan's court ring with the news that Joseph's brothers are come, that the saints are arrived safe at the bosom of Christ, out of the reach of hell for ever. . . . Know this, believer, to your everlasting comfort, if those arms have once embraced you, neither sin nor hell can get you away for ever.

You are not dealing with an inconstant creature, but with Him with whom is no variableness nor shadow of turning. His love for you will not be as yours was on earth to him–seldom, and cold, up, and down. He that would not cease nor abate his love, for all your enmity, unkind neglects, and churlish resistances–can he cease to love you, when he has made you truly lovely?
–Richard Baxter

**RICHARD BAXTER**
**(1615-1691)**

He left London as a teenager, disillusioned with English rule and religion, and joined the ranks of the Nonconformists. Though he was made chaplain to Charles II after the Restoration, his revision of the *Book of Common Prayer* brought him under fire when the Act of Uniformity restored the Anglican establishment to complete control of the church in 1662. Excluded from church leadership, he was imprisoned twice for daring to preach, but continued to fight for the cause of religious tolerance.

# Change in Your Diet

COMPARED TO THE FRENCH FRIES AND DOUGHNUTS OF THE WORLD, CHRISTIANITY'S FRESH
FRUITS AND SALADS CAN SEEM A LITTLE ON THE . . . WELL, BORING SIDE. BUT SURELY BY NOW,
WE'VE BEEN BURNED BY ENOUGH DRIVE-THROUGH SHOOTING PAINS OF HEARTACHE AND REGRET
TO KNOW THAT THE WORLD'S OFFERINGS COST A LOT MORE THAN THE THREE DOLLARS AND
CHANGE THEY ADVERTISE UP FRONT. HAVEN'T WE?

## Isaiah 55:1-2, 6-7, 12a, 13

"Come, all you who are thirsty, come to the waters; and you who
have no money, come, buy and eat! Come, buy wine and milk without money and without cost.

"Why spend money on what is not bread, and your labor on what
does not satisfy? Listen, listen to me, and eat what is good, and your
soul will delight in the richest of fare. . . .

"Seek the LORD while he may be found; call on him while he is
near. Let the wicked forsake his way and the evil man his thoughts.
Let him turn to the LORD, and he will have mercy on him, and to our
God, for he will freely pardon. . . .

"You will go out in joy and be led forth in peace. . . . Instead of
the thornbush will grow the pine tree, and instead of briers the myr-
tle will grow. This will be for the LORD's renown, for an everlasting
sign, which will not be destroyed."

PERSONALLY SPEAKING *Pick out one of your bad habits today. And ask God to
show you what He can give you in place of the junk. Want to keep your spirit
healthy? Watch what you feed it.*

Righteousness is the natural and essential food of the soul, which can no more be satisfied by earthly treasures than the hunger of the body can be satisfied by air. If you should see a starving man standing with mouth open to the wind, inhaling drafts of air as if in hope of gratifying his hunger, you would think him lunatic. But it is no less foolish to imagine that the soul can be satisfied with worldly things which only inflate it without feeding it.

What have spiritual gifts to do with carnal appetites, or carnal with spiritual? He bestows bounty immeasurable; He provokes thee to good, He preserves thee in goodness; He prevents, He sustains, He fills thee. He moves thee to longing, and it is He for whom thou longest.

The motive for loving God is God Himself. . . . He is such that love to Him is a natural due . . . Our love is prepared and rewarded by His. He loves us first, out of His great tenderness; then we are bound to repay Him with love; and we are permitted to cherish exultant hopes in Him. . . .

He has no gift better than Himself. He gives Himself as prize and reward: He is the refreshment of the holy soul, the ransom of those in captivity.
–Bernard of Clairvaux

BERNARD OF
CLAIRVAUX
(1090-1153)

As a young French abbot of only twenty-five, Bernard established a monastic community in Clairvaux which soon became the order's principal center. He was known at first for his firm belief in strict disciplinary observance, yet his theology softened in later years from an emphasis on God's judgment to His infinite love and mercy. In addition to his sermons and treatises, several hymns are attributed to him: "Jesus, the Very Thought of Thee," "O Sacred Head, Now Wounded," and "Jesus, Thou Joy of Loving Hearts."

# TO SAVE YOUR SKIN

EVERYBODY KNOWS THEY'RE SUPPOSED TO BE UNSELFISH, MORE CONCERNED ABOUT GOD AND OTHERS. ISN'T IT FUNNY, THOUGH, THAT GOD'S APPEAL FOR OUR SOULS PLAYS RIGHT INTO OUR SELF-INTERESTS—OUR FEAR OF DEATH, OUR AVOIDANCE OF PUNISHMENT, OUR CRAVING FOR IMMORTALITY. PERHAPS GOD'S NOT AS OFFENDED AS YOU MIGHT EXPECT WHEN PEOPLE COME TO HIM WANTING FIRE INSURANCE.

## Acts 16:25-32

*About midnight Paul and Silas were praying and singing hymns to God, and the other prisoners were listening to them. Suddenly there was such a violent earthquake that the foundations of the prison were shaken. At once all the prison doors flew open, and everybody's chains came loose.*

*The jailer woke up, and when he saw the prison doors open, he drew his sword and was about to kill himself because he thought the prisoners had escaped. But Paul shouted, "Don't harm yourself! We are all here!"*

*The jailer called for lights, rushed in and fell trembling before Paul and Silas. He then brought them out and asked, "Sirs, what must I do to be saved?"*

*They replied, "Believe in the Lord Jesus, and you will be saved—you and your household." Then they spoke the word of the Lord to him and to all the others in his house.*

PERSONALLY SPEAKING *Before you take the hellfire out of your witnessing weaponry, remember that being scared into heaven isn't the worst thing that could happen to your friends and family.*

_____

_____

_____

_____

_____

_____

You have gone in quest of salvation from a sense of danger, or fear of the wrath to come, or a desire to obtain the inheritance of glory. How could it be otherwise? God made you with these fears and hopes; and he appeals to them in his word. When he says, "Turn ye, turn ye, for why will ye die?" he is appealing to your fears. When he sets eternal life before you, and the joys of an endless kingdom, he is appealing to your hopes. And when he presents these motives, he expects you to be moved by them. To act upon such motives, then, cannot be wrong. Nay, not to act upon them, would be to harden yourself against God's most solemn appeals. . . .

Do not keep back from Christ under the idea that you must come to him in a disinterested frame, and from an unselfish motive. If you were right in this thing, who could be saved? You are to come as you are; with all your bad motives, whatever these may be. Take all your bad motives, add them to the number of your sins, and bring them all to the altar where the great sacrifice is lying. Go to the mercy seat. Tell the High Priest there, not what you desire to be, nor what you ought to be, but what you are. . . . He wants you to come to Him exactly as you are, and not to cherish the vain thought that, by a little waiting, or working, or praying, you can make yourself fit, or persuade Him to make you fit.
–Horatius Bonar

HORATIUS
BONAR
(1808-1889)

"The prince of Scottish hymnwriters" began preaching in 1837, and by 1843 had joined with other evangelicals during the "Great Disruption" to form the new Free Church of Scotland. By this time, he had also started to write hymns, which would total over six hundred in his lifetime, at first setting Christian words to familiar tunes to interest children in worship. For twenty years he helped arrange D. L. Moody's meetings in Edinburgh, and he continued his own preaching ministry until nearly eighty years of age.

# COSTLY DISCIPLESHIP

SOMETIMES WE DON'T NEED ANOTHER CHANCE TO EXPRESS HOW WE FEEL OR TO ASK SOMEONE TO UNDERSTAND OUR SITUATION. SOMETIMES WE JUST NEED A FIRM KICK IN THE PANTS, AN UNSMILING EXPECTATION THAT IF WE MEAN ALL THESE WONDERFUL THINGS WE TALK ABOUT AND SING ABOUT, THEN LET'S SEE SOMETHING TO PROVE IT. DON'T BE COMING BACK IN HERE WITH ALL YOUR EXCUSES. IS THAT CLEAR?

## Mark 10:23-25, 28-31

Jesus looked around and said to his disciples, "How hard it is for the rich to enter the kingdom of God!"

The disciples were amazed at his words. But Jesus said again, "Children, how hard it is to enter the kingdom of God! It is easier for a camel to go through the eye of a needle than for a rich man to enter the kingdom of God. . . ."

Peter said to him, "We have left everything to follow you!"

"I tell you the truth," Jesus replied, "no one who has left home or brothers or sisters or mother or father or children or fields for me and the gospel will fail to receive a hundred times as much in this present age (homes, brothers, sisters, mothers, children and fields—and with them, persecutions) and in the age to come, eternal life. But many who are first will be last, and the last first."

PERSONALLY SPEAKING *Where are you in the discipleship department? Are you actively studying the Bible, growing in prayer, holding yourself accountable to live what you believe? There's no good reason not to.*

_____

_____

_____

_____

_____

_____

The gracious call of Jesus now becomes a stern command: Do this! Give up that! Leave the ship and come to me! When a man says he cannot obey the call of Jesus because he believes, or because he does not believe, Jesus says: "First obey, perform the external work, renounce your attachments, give up the obstacles which separate you from the will of God. Do not say you have not got faith. You will not have it so long as you persist in disobedience and refuse to take the first step. You have not got faith so long as and because you will not take the first step but become hardened in your unbelief under the guise of humble faith."

It is a malicious subterfuge to argue like this, a sure sign of lack of faith, which leads in its turn to a lack of obedience. This is the disobedience of the "believers"—when they are asked to obey, they simply confess their unbelief and leave it at that.

You are trifling with the subject. If you believe, take the first step, it leads to Jesus Christ. If you don't believe, take the first step all the same, for you are bidden to take it. No one wants to know about your faith or unbelief, your orders are to perform the act of obedience on the spot. Then you will find yourself in the situation where faith becomes possible and where faith exists in the true sense of the word.

–Dietrich Bonhoeffer

DIETRICH
BONHOEFFER
(1906-1945)

He was dead at thirty-nine, a Lutheran pastor and son of a famous German neurologist who dared like few others to believe he had a duty to oppose Nazi ideology. His license to teach in his own seminary was revoked in 1936; Himmler shut down the seminary in 1937. And in April 1943, he was arrested by the Gestapo for his part in the Resistance movement. Two years later he was executed on a charge of treason, leaving behind a brave legacy of courage and conviction. And living proof of *The Cost of Discipleship*.

# LOVE'S DIRTY HANDS

WE TEND TO PREFER LOVE WHEN IT LOOKS LIKE SUNSETS AND PICNICS, WHEN IT SMELLS OF COR-
NER BAKERIES AND ROSE PETALS. BUT SOMETIMES LOVE MEANS GRASPING THE HARD, LEATHERY
HANDS OF POVERTY WITHOUT WORRYING HOW MANY GERMS THEY'RE CARRYING, IGNORING THE
SOURED LINEN OF THE NURSING HOME WARD, SO THAT GOD'S LOVE CAN FRESHEN THE HEARTS
OF HIS CHILDREN. THROUGH YOUR LOVE.

### *Isaiah 53:2b-5, 8b, 12*

*He had no beauty or majesty to attract us to him, nothing in his
appearance that we should desire him. He was despised and rejected
by men, a man of sorrows, and familiar with suffering. Like one from
whom men hide their faces he was despised, and we esteemed him
not.*

*Surely he took up our infirmities and carried our sorrows, yet we
considered him stricken by God, smitten by him, and afflicted. But he
was pierced for our transgressions, he was crushed for our iniquities;
the punishment that brought us peace was upon him, and by his
wounds we are healed. . . .*

*For he was cut off from the land of the living; for the transgres-
sion of my people he was stricken. . . .*

*Therefore I will give him a portion among the great, and he will
divide the spoils with the strong, because he poured out his life unto
death, and was numbered with the transgressors. For he bore the sin
of many, and made intercession for the transgressors.*

PERSONALLY SPEAKING *God is calling you to serve. And you know it. Why
wait another week to begin doing that thing He's been laying on your heart? You
never look more dignified to God than when you're loving others.*

Oh, precious Savior! Save us from maligning Your Gospel and Your name by clothing it with our paltry notions of earthly dignity, and forgetting the dignity which crowned Your sacred brow as You hung upon the cross! That is the dignity for us, and it will never suffer by any gentleman here carrying the Gospel into the back slums or alleys of any town or city in which he lives. That dignity will never suffer by any employer talking lovingly to his servant maid or errand boy, and looking into his eyes with tears of sympathy and love, and trying to bring his soul to Jesus.

That dignity will never suffer, even though you should have to be dragged through the streets with a howling mob at your heels, like Jesus Christ, if you have gone into those streets for the soul of your fellowmen and the glory of God. Though you should be tied to a stake, as were the martyrs of old, and surrounded by laughing and taunting friends and their howling followers–that will be a dignity which shall be crowned in heaven, crowned with everlasting glory. If I understand it, that is the dignity of the Gospel–the dignity of love. I do not envy, I do not covet any other. I desire no other–God is my witness–than the dignity of love.
–Catherine Booth

CATHERINE
BOOTH
(1829-1890)

When she was a young adult, her congregation expelled her for her religious zeal, along with its pastor–the man she would marry in 1855. She had eight children along the way, but as a gifted preacher in her own right, she joined her husband, William, on his many evangelistic travels. Together, motivated by the poverty and hardship they encountered on their journeys, they originated the Christian Mission in London's East End, which would grow into a worldwide movement known as . . . the Salvation Army.

# LET US PRAY

WHEN YOU'RE IN TOO BIG A HURRY IN THE MORNING, YOU CAN SURVIVE OFF LAST NIGHT'S SUP-
PER TILL LUNCHTIME. IN A PINCH, YOU MAY EVEN BE ABLE TO GO WITHOUT A SHAVE OR BE
FORCED TO LIVE WITH A RUN IN YOUR HOSE. BUT YESTERDAY'S PRAYER WAS FOR YESTERDAY'S
PROBLEMS, AND IT WON'T BE ENOUGH FOR TODAY'S NEW DEVELOPMENTS. THERE'S A NEW DAY
IN PRAYER. AND THAT DAY IS RIGHT NOW.

## Matthew 6:25-27, 31-34

"Therefore I tell you, do not worry about your life, what you will
eat or drink; or about your body, what you will wear. Is not life more
important than food, and the body more important than clothes?

"Look at the birds of the air; they do not sow or reap or store
away in barns, and yet your heavenly Father feeds them. Are you not
much more valuable than they? Who of you by worrying can add a
single hour to his life? . . .

"So do not worry, saying, 'What shall we eat?' or 'What shall we
drink?' or 'What shall we wear?' For the pagans run after all these
things, and your heavenly Father knows that you need them.

"But seek first his kingdom and his righteousness, and all these
things will be given to you as well.

"Therefore do not worry about tomorrow, for tomorrow will
worry about itself. Each day has enough trouble of its own.

PERSONALLY SPEAKING *Before breakfast, before the paper, before the traffic
report, there's something God needs to go over with you. It's about your day. And
you don't really want it in your own hands.*

_____

_____

_____

_____

_____

_____

True prayers are born of present trials and needs. Bread, for today, is bread enough. Bread given for today is the strongest sort of pledge that there will be bread tomorrow. Victory today is the assurance of victory tomorrow. Our prayers need to be focused upon the present. We must trust God today, and leave the morrow entirely with Him. The present is ours; the future belongs to God. Prayer is the task and duty of each recurring day of daily prayer for daily needs.

As every day demands its bread, so every day demands its prayer. No amount of praying, done today, will suffice for tomorrow's praying. On the other hand, no praying for tomorrow is of any great value to us today. Today's manna is what we need; tomorrow God will see that our needs are supplied. This is the faith which God seeks to inspire. So leave tomorrow, with its cares, its needs, its troubles, in God's hands. There is no storing tomorrow's grace or tomorrow's praying; neither is there any laying-up of today's grace, to meet tomorrow's necessities. We cannot have tomorrow's grace, we cannot eat tomorrow's bread, we cannot do tomorrow's praying. "Sufficient unto the day is the evil thereof"; and, most assuredly, if we possess faith, sufficient also will be the good.
–E. M. Bounds

E. M. BOUNDS
(1835-1913)

Born in Missouri, he practiced for three years as a lawyer before surrendering to preach in the Methodist Episcopal Church South. Duty called him into the Civil War, however, where he served as a captain in the Confederacy. The war over, he returned to the pulpit, serving churches in Tennessee, Alabama, and Missouri, where he became editor of the *St. Louis Christian Advocate*. But he didn't write his widely read devotional books until the last years of his life, free from the daily demands of the pastorate.

# THE GLORY OF HIS PRESENCE

YOU CAN FAITHFULLY PRAY INTO THE CEILING FOR DAYS, WEEKS, MONTHS, BELIEVING IN FAITH THAT GOD IS HEARING AND RESPONDING, REMEMBERING THAT YOU'RE DOWN HERE, NOT FORGETTING HIS PROMISES TO HEAL, PROTECT, AND PROVIDE. BUT WHEN GOD KNOWS YOU NEED IT, HE'LL PART THE CURTAIN FOR A WHILE AND OPEN YOUR SPIRITUAL EYES TO THE JOYS OF ANOTHER WORLD. JUST WAIT TILL YOU SEE.

## Psalm 24:3-6; 16:2, 7-11

*Who may ascend the hill of the LORD? Who may stand in his holy place? He who has clean hands and a pure heart, who does not lift up his soul to an idol or swear by what is false. He will receive blessing from the LORD and vindication from God his Savior. Such is the generation of those who seek him, who seek your face, O God of Jacob....*

*I said to the LORD, "You are my LORD; apart from you I have no good thing"....I will praise the LORD, who counsels me; even at night my heart instructs me.*

*I have set the LORD always before me. Because he is at my right hand, I will not be shaken. Therefore my heart is glad and my tongue rejoices; my body also will rest secure, because you will not abandon me to the grave, nor will you let your Holy One see decay.*

*You have made known to me the path of life; you will fill me with joy in your presence, with eternal pleasures at your right hand.*

PERSONALLY SPEAKING *Come back to God in prayer today, even if it's been a while since you had the feeling you were getting through. Stay thankful. Keep praising. And who knows what He might show you?*

_____

_____

_____

_____

_____

_____

Lord's Day, April 25. At night I was exceedingly melted with divine love and had some feeling sense of the blessedness of the upper world. Those words hung upon me with much divine sweetness, Psalm 84:7: "They go from strength to strength, every one of them in Zion appeareth before God."

Oh, the near access that God sometimes gives us in our addresses to Him! This may well be termed appearing before God: it is so indeed, in the true spiritual sense, and in the sweetest sense. I think I have not had such power of intercession these many months, both for God's children and for dead sinners as I have had this evening. I wished and longed for the coming of my dear Lord: I longed to join the angelic hosts in praises, wholly free from imperfections.

Oh, the blessed moment hastens! All I want is to be more holy, more like my dear Lord. Oh, for sanctification! My very soul pants for the complete restoration of the blessed image of my Savior, that I may be fit for the blessed enjoyments and employments of the heavenly world.

Oh, the new Jerusalem; my soul longed for it. Oh, the song of Moses and the Lamb! And that blessed song that no man can learn but they who are redeemed from the earth, and the glorious white robes that were given to the souls under the altar!

–David Brainerd

**DAVID BRAINERD**
(1718-1747)

He was profoundly converted at age twenty-one, and several years later was even expelled from Yale for misdemeanors arising from his "intemperate, indiscreet zeal." He was forced, then, to study privately, but received a license to preach and accepted an appointment as missionary to the Indians in eastern Pennsylvania. By 1745 he had ridden over three thousand miles on horseback, seeing dozens of Indians saved, but succumbing himself to the ravages of disease and hardship. He died at the home of Jonathan Edwards.

# ALWAYS ON TIME

YOU LEARN WHAT TO EXPECT FROM PEOPLE WHO ARE ALWAYS RUNNING LATE. TEN MINUTES PAST? THEY'LL BE HERE. HALF AN HOUR LATE? JUST KEEP THEIR PLATE WARM IN THE OVEN. AND WHEN THEY FINALLY SHOW UP, THERE ARE THE USUAL APOLOGIES, THE STANDARD JOKES, THE STOCK ONE-LINERS. BUT IF WE CAN LEARN TO TRUST IN PEOPLE WHO ARE NEVER ON TIME, WHY IS IT SO HARD TO TRUST GOD, WHO'S ALWAYS ON TIME?

### Philippians 4:6-7; Matthew 10:29-31; Psalm 145:15-19

Do not be anxious about anything, but in everything, by prayer and petition, with thanksgiving, present your requests to God. And the peace of God, which transcends all understanding, will guard your hearts and your minds in Christ Jesus. . . .

Are not two sparrows sold for a penny? Yet not one of them will fall to the ground apart from the will of your Father. And even the very hairs of your head are all numbered. So don't be afraid; you are worth more than many sparrows. . . .

The eyes of all look to you, and you give them their food at the proper time. You open your hand and satisfy the desires of every living thing. The LORD is righteous in all his ways and loving toward all he has made. The LORD is near to all who call on him, to all who call on him in truth. He fulfills the desires of those who fear him; he hears their cry and saves them.

PERSONALLY SPEAKING *Been praying about something a long time? And waiting for what's starting to seem like forever? Try to rest in the fact that God knows what He's doing. He'll be here. And not a minute too late.*

God's commissary department is abundantly full and runs on schedule time, but the worried and anxious unbeliever wants Him to run ahead of schedule time. No, no! He may, in order to test and strengthen faith, not provide the second suit until the first one is ready to be laid aside, and sometimes after supper he may allow you to go to bed not knowing where the breakfast is to come from, but it will come at breakfast time.

"He knows that you have need of these things," so trust Him, as does the sparrow. The wee thing tucks its tiny head under its little wing and sleeps, not knowing where it will find its breakfast, and when the day dawns it chirps its merry note of praise, and God opens His great hand and feeds it. "The eyes of all wait upon you and you give them their meat in due season. You open your hand and satisfy the desire of every living thing," said the Psalmist (Psalm 145:15, 16), and "You are of more value than many sparrows."

O my anxious brother, trust Him! He will not fail you. In this, as in all other things, the assurance holds good, that there hath no temptation taken you but such as is common to man; but God is faithful, who will not suffer you to be tempted above that ye are able, but will with the temptation make a way of escape that ye may be able to bear it. (1 Corinthians 10:13) Hallelujah! I have proved this in times past, and I may have to prove it again, but "God is faithful." And the devil is a liar and always will be.

–Samuel Logan Brengle

SAMUEL LOGAN
BRENGLE
(1860-1936)

He served in the Salvation Army for more than forty years, but not before the Army's founder, William Booth, had admonished him to seek another ministry, convinced he could never submit to its discipline. But while cleaning boots in a dingy cellar, Brengle had a chance to assess whether he was wasting his talents, and was quickened by the thought of Christ washing the disciple's feet. "That experience put a key in my hand to unlock the hearts of lowly people all around the world for the next forty years!"

# KNOWN BY LOVE

PEOPLE OUTSIDE DON'T REALLY CARE SO MUCH ABOUT WHERE WE STAND ON PREDESTINATION, OR HOW MANY SERVICES WE HAVE ON SUNDAY, OR WHAT MUSIC WE'RE SINGING THIS EASTER. THOSE ARE JUST THE LEAVES ON OUR SPIRITUAL TREE. BUT WHEN THEY SEE PEOPLE WHO LOVE EACH OTHER, WHO KNOW EACH OTHER'S FAULTS BUT STILL ENJOY EACH OTHER'S COMPANY, THEY DISCOVER THERE'S FRUIT ON THESE BRANCHES.

## 1 John 4:13, 16–21

*We know that we live in him and he in us, because he has given us of his Spirit. . . . And so we know and rely on the love God has for us. God is love. Whoever lives in love lives in God, and God in him.*

*In this way, love is made complete among us so that we will have confidence on the day of judgment, because in this world we are like him.*

*There is no fear in love. But perfect love drives out fear, because fear has to do with punishment. The one who fears is not made perfect in love.*

*We love because he first loved us. If anyone says, "I love God," yet hates his brother, he is a liar. For anyone who does not love his brother, whom he has seen, cannot love God, whom he has not seen.*

*And he has given us this command: Whoever loves God must also love his brother.*

PERSONALLY SPEAKING *Of all the things you stay busy with at church, how much of your time do you invest in other people? Causes are noble. Classes are productive. But love is what reaches the world.*

We now come to speak of love, which, I said, joins together the members of the body ecclesiastical mutually among themselves.

The Lord says in the Gospel: "A new commandment give I unto you, that ye love one another." There is therefore no doubt that after faith the only mark of the Church is love, a bond which most firmly knits together all the members.

It grows from the communion of Christ and unity of the Spirit. For since Christ, the king, the head and high bishop of the Church, enduing us all with one and the same Spirit, has made us all his members, the sons of God, brethren and fellow-heirs, whom without doubt he tenderly loves, the faithful man can only with fervent love embrace the members and fellow-heirs of their king, their head and their high bishop. . . . Between the highest members of the Church and the lowest, there is a great and fitting agreement, and also a diligent care and assistance which is both continual and most faithful.

From all this it appears that the marks of the true and lively Church of Christ are the communion of the Spirit of Christ, sincere faith, and Christian charity, without which no man is a partaker of this spiritual body. And by these things you may easily judge whether you are in the fellowship of the Church or not.

–Heinrich Bullinger

HEINRICH
BULLINGER
(1504-1575)

He was born the son of a parish priest in a small town in Switzerland, but was moved during his college years toward the Reform movements that were finding their leading voice in another Swiss preacher, Ulrich Zwingli. Forced from his home as a result of the Second Kappel War, he fled to Zurich, where the Council installed him as Zwingli's successor at the Zurich Great Church. His ministry was marked by conciliatory alliances with Calvin and other Reformers that broadened the base of the movement.

# STOPPING SUBTLE SIN

YOU WOULDN'T THINK GOD COULD BRUISE THAT EASILY. YOU WOULDN'T THINK A GOD WHO CAN CARVE OUT OCEANS WITH HIS THUMBPRINTS AND KNOCK APOSTLE PAULS TO THE GROUND COULD SPEAK WITH SUCH A STILL, SMALL VOICE. YOU WOULDN'T THINK THAT GIVING IN TO A WEAK HABIT JUST THIS ONE TIME WOULD MATTER ALL THAT MUCH . . . TO YOU OR TO HIM. BUT IF OUR SIN HURTS GOD, JUST THINK WHAT IT DOES TO US.

## *Ephesians 4:22-27, 30; 5:15-17*

*You were taught, with regard to your former way of life, to put off your old self, which is being corrupted by its deceitful desires; to be made new in the attitude of your minds; and to put on the new self, created to be like God in true righteousness and holiness.*

*Therefore each of you must put off falsehood and speak truthfully to his neighbor, for we are all members of one body. "In your anger do not sin": Do not let the sun go down while you are still angry, and do not give the devil a foothold. . . .*

*And do not grieve the Holy Spirit of God, with whom you were sealed for the day of redemption. . . .*

*Be very careful, then, how you live—not as unwise but as wise, making the most of every opportunity, because the days are evil. Therefore do not be foolish, but understand what the Lord's will is.*

PERSONALLY SPEAKING *It's not worth it. Whatever the devil's teasing you with today, whatever kind of amnesia has made you forget how sorry you were before, it's a lie. Don't you even think about it.*

We that religiously name the name of Christ should depart from iniquity, because the Spirit of the Father will else be grieved. The countenancing of iniquity, the not departing therefrom, will grieve the Holy Spirit of God, by which you are sealed to the day of redemption: and that is a sin of a higher nature than men commonly are aware of.

He that grieveth the Spirit of God shall smart for it here, or in hell, or both. . . . He that grieves the Spirit, quenches it, and he that quenches it, vexes it; and he that vexes it, sets it against himself, and tempts it to hasten destruction upon himself. Wherefore take heed, you that religiously name the name of Christ, that you meddle not with iniquity, that you tempt not the Spirit of the Lord to do such things against you. . . .

A man knows not whither he is going, nor where he shall stop, that is but entering into temptation; nor whether he shall ever turn back, or go out at the gap that is right before him. He that has begun to grieve the Holy Ghost, may be suffered to go on until he has sinned that sin which is called the sin against the Holy Ghost. And if God shall once give you up to that, then you are in an iron cage, out of which there is neither deliverance nor redemption. Let every one, therefore, that nameth the name of Christ, depart from iniquity.
–John Bunyan

JOHN BUNYAN
(1628-1688)

He was a foul-mouthed rogue who could neither read nor write, until his new bride introduced him to Puritan books and forced him to clean up his life. Within a couple of years, he was preaching the Gospel in Bedford, England, when the magistrate arrested him for preaching without a government license. Imprisoned off and on from 1660 to 1672, he wrote (among others) his famous *Pilgrim's Progress*, which along with the Bible and *Foxe's Book of Martyrs* was read in virtually every Victorian home.

# THE PERFECT GENTLEMAN

NOBODY YOU KNOW HAS IT ALL TOGETHER. PEOPLE ARE STRONG IN DIFFERENT WAYS. THOSE WHO CAN CAPTIVATE YOUR MINDS WITH THEIR PROFOUND UNDERSTANDING MAY NOT BE WILLING TO HELP YOU MOVE NEXT SATURDAY. THOSE WHO ARE QUICK TO TAKE A LOOK AT YOUR RADIATOR LEAK MAY NOT BE COMFORTABLE PRAYING WITH YOU. BUT GOD, OUR GOD, IS EVERYTHING GOOD, TAKEN TO THE ULTIMATE EXTREME.

## *Isaiah 49:8-11, 13; 40:11a*

*This is what the LORD says: "In the time of my favor I will answer you, and in the day of salvation I will help you; I will keep you and will make you to be a covenant for the people, to restore the land and to reassign its desolate inheritances, to say to the captives, 'Come out,' and to those in darkness, 'Be free!'*

*"They will feed beside the roads and find pasture on every barren hill. They will neither hunger nor thirst, nor will the desert heat or the sun beat upon them. He who has compassion on them will guide them and lead them beside springs of water. I will turn all my mountains into roads, and my highways will be raised up. . . ."*

*Shout for joy, O heavens; rejoice, O earth; burst into song, O mountains! For the LORD comforts his people and will have compassion on his afflicted ones. . . . He tends his flock like a shepherd: He gathers the lambs in his arms and carries them close to his heart.*

PERSONALLY SPEAKING *Whatever kind of father has been modeled to you on earth, be confident of this: Your Father in heaven is gentle and kind, caring and compassionate. You have no idea how much He loves you.*

Gentleness in a deity–what other religion ever took up such a thought? When the coarse mind of sin makes up gods and a religion by its own natural light, the gods reveal both the coarseness and the sin together, as they properly should. They are made great as being great in force, and terrible in their resentments. They are mounted on tigers, hung about with snakes, cleave the sea with tridents, pound the sky with thunders, blow tempests out of their cheeks, send murrain upon the cattle, and pestilence on the cities and kingdoms of other gods–always raging in some lust or jealousy, or scaring the world by some vengeful portent.

Just opposite to all these, the great God and creator of the world, the God of revelation, the God and Father of our Lord Jesus Christ, contrives to be a gentle being; even hiding his power, and withholding the stress of his will, that he may put confidence and courage in the feeling of his children. Let us not shrink then from the epithet of Scripture, as if it must imply some derogation from God's real greatness and majesty; for we are much more likely to reach the impression, before we have done, that precisely here do his greatness and majesty culminate.

–Horace Bushnell

HORACE
BUSHNELL
(1802-1876)

After graduating from Yale in 1827, passing all his examinations, and preparing for admission to the bar, he was convicted to the heart during a revival at the college and suddenly decided to enter the divinity school. He was ordained as pastor of the North Church of Hartford in 1833, where he remained until ill health forced him to resign the pulpit in 1859. His major written works espoused three cardinal pieces of his theology: *Christian Nurture, Nature and Supernatural,* and *The Vicarious Sacrifice.*

# ALL YOU'LL EVER NEED

EVEN IN THIS DAY OF MEGA-MALLS AND SUPERSTORES, WHERE YOU CAN GET BREAKFAST CEREAL AND SNOW TIRES WITHOUT HAVING TO HUNT FOR A NEW PARKING SPACE, YOU STILL CAN'T REALLY GET EVERYTHING YOU WANT IN ONE SPOT. LIFE STILL REQUIRES SOME DRIVING AROUND TOWN. BUT NOT YOUR SPIRITUAL LIFE. WHATEVER YOU NEED, WHATEVER'S REQUIRED, JESUS CHRIST HAS A FULL SUPPLY. SAVE YOURSELF A SIDE TRIP.

## Colossians 1:13-20

For he has rescued us from the dominion of darkness and brought us into the kingdom of the Son he loves, in whom we have redemption, the forgiveness of sins.

He is the image of the invisible God, the firstborn over all creation. For by him all things were created: things in heaven and on earth, visible and invisible, whether thrones or powers or rulers or authorities; all things were created by him and for him.

He is before all things, and in him all things hold together. And he is the head of the body, the church; he is the beginning and the firstborn from among the dead, so that in everything he might have the supremacy.

For God was pleased to have all his fullness dwell in him, and through him to reconcile to himself all things, whether things on earth or things in heaven, by making peace through his blood, shed on the cross.

PERSONALLY SPEAKING *If you've been looking for real encouragement, genuine peace, authentic willpower, only one place carries them. In fact, there's one in your neighborhood. And it's open right now.*

We see that our whole salvation and all its parts are comprehended in Christ. We should therefore take care not to derive the least portion of it from anywhere else. If we seek salvation, we are taught by the very name of Jesus that it is "of him." If we seek any other gifts of the Spirit, they will be found in his anointing.

If we seek strength, it lies in his dominion; if purity, in his conception; if gentleness, it appears in his birth. For by his birth he was made like us in all respects that he might learn to feel our pain.

If we seek redemption, it lies in his passion; if acquittal, in his condemnation; if remission of the curse, in his cross; if satisfaction, in his sacrifice; if purification, in his blood; if reconciliation, in his descent into hell; if mortification of the flesh, in his tomb; if newness of life, in his resurrection; if immortality, in the same; if inheritance of the Heavenly Kingdom, in his entrance into heaven; if protection, if security, if abundant supply of all blessings, in his Kingdom; if untroubled expectation of judgment, in the power given to him to judge. In short, since rich store of every kind of good abounds in him, let us drink our fill from this fountain, and from no other.

–John Calvin

**JOHN CALVIN**
**(1509-1564)**

In France, his early Protestant writings forced him to stay on the move to avoid arrest. But when Reform began losing steam in Geneva, Switzerland—and a change in government put control in the hands of friends who encouraged his help—he embraced the opportunity, revising church government, establishing a system of education to perpetuate his aims, and encouraging government care for the poor and the aged. At fifty-four, this dominant figure of the Reformation died, literally burned out in God's service.

# A Cause for Comfort

WHEN YOU'RE HURTING, ALL YOU CAN FEEL IS YOUR OWN PAIN. WHEN YOU'RE DISCOURAGED, ALL YOU CAN SENSE IS YOUR OWN FAILURE. WHEN YOU'RE LONELY, ALL YOU CAN THINK ABOUT IS YOUR OWN EMPTINESS. BUT IN THE DARK PASSAGEWAYS OF PERSONAL PAIN, GOD CAN TURN YOUR NATURAL CONCERN FOR YOURSELF INTO A RECEPTIVE UNDERSTANDING FOR OTHERS. AND HEALING CAN COME FULL CIRCLE.

## 2 Corinthians 1:3-7, 10b-11

Praise be to the God and Father of our Lord Jesus Christ, the Father of compassion and the God of all comfort, who comforts us in all our troubles, so that we can comfort those in any trouble with the comfort we ourselves have received from God.

For just as the sufferings of Christ flow over into our lives, so also through Christ our comfort overflows.

If we are distressed, it is for your comfort and salvation; if we are comforted, it is for your comfort, which produces in you patient endurance of the same sufferings we suffer. And our hope for you is firm, because we know that just as you share in our sufferings, so also you share in our comfort. . . .

On him we have set our hope that he will continue to deliver us, as you help us by your prayers. Then many will give thanks on our behalf for the gracious favor granted us in answer to the prayers of many.

PERSONALLY SPEAKING *Give some thought to this idea: One reason God extends His comfort to you is so that you can in turn extend it to others. You've been there. Are you doing that?*

_____

_____

_____

_____

_____

_____

But to what end is pain? I do not clearly know. But I have noticed that when one who has not suffered draws near to one in pain, there is rarely much power to help. There is not the understanding that leaves the suffering thing comforted, though perhaps not a word was spoken.

I have wondered if it can be the same in the sphere of prayer. Does pain accepted and endured give some quality that would otherwise be lacking in prayer? Does it create sympathy which can lay itself alongside the need, feeling it as though it were personal, so that it is possible to do just what the writer of Hebrews meant when he said, "Remember them that are in bonds, as bound with them, and them which suffer adversity, as being yourselves also in the body" (Hebrews 13:3)?

What if every stroke of pain, or hour of weariness or loneliness, or any other trial of flesh or spirit, could carry us a pulsebeat nearer some other life, some life for which the ministry of prayer is needed; would it not be worthwhile to suffer? Ten thousand times yes. And surely it must be so, for the further we are drawn into the fellowship of Calvary with our dear Lord, the tenderer we are toward others, the closer alongside does our spirit lie with them that are in bonds; as being ourselves also in the body. God never wastes His children's pain.

–Amy Carmichael

AMY
CARMICHAEL
(1867-1951)

After working in Japan for a short time, she set her sights on South India in 1895, where she began the Dohnavur Fellowship, a Christian ministry dedicated to rescuing young girls from temple prostitution. She maintained active leadership over this stark outreach until 1931, when a fall led to crippling arthritis and confined her to her bed for the final twenty years of her life. Still, she remained at the center of the Fellowship's ministry, inspiring many with her devotional books and poems until her death in 1951.

# SEEING YOU THROUGH

IF YOU WERE TO STAND BACK AND LOOK AT YOUR LIFE FROM A COMFORTABLE DISTANCE, ANA-
LYZING IT WITH THE SAME OBJECTIVE HINDSIGHT YOU USE WHEN READING A HISTORY BOOK, SEE-
ING THE DANGERS THAT COULD HAVE OCCURRED IF A SMALL MISSTEP HAD BEEN MADE HERE OR
A MINOR DECISION CHANGED THERE, YOU'D WONDER HOW YOU'D BEEN ABLE TO NAVIGATE IT.
YOU'D KNOW IT WASN'T REALLY YOU.

## Psalm 106:9-12; Isaiah 63:11-14

He rebuked the Red Sea, and it dried up; he led them through the
depths as through a desert. He saved them from the hand of the foe;
from the hand of the enemy he redeemed them. The waters covered
their adversaries; not one of them survived. Then they believed his
promises and sang his praise. . . .

Then his people recalled the days of old, the days of Moses and
his people—where is he who brought them through the sea, with the
shepherd of his flock? Where is he who set his Holy Spirit among
them, who sent his glorious arm of power to be at Moses' right hand,
who divided the waters before them, to gain for himself everlasting
renown, who led them through the depths?

Like a horse in open country, they did not stumble; like cattle
that go down to the plain, they were given rest by the Spirit of the
LORD. This is how you guided your people to make for yourself a glorious name.

PERSONALLY SPEAKING *Try not to think about it—all the eventualities of life
that hinge on even the smallest decisions you make. Why drive yourself crazy
with what-ifs when you're in such good hands with God?*

_____

_____

_____

_____

_____

_____

There is nothing more certain to resist the wiles of the flesh than simplicity. Divine action can make simple souls take exactly the right steps to surprise those who wish to surprise them, and even to profit by their attempts to do so. They are buoyed up by humiliation, every vexation becomes a blessing, and by leaving their adversaries alone, they derive such a lasting and satisfactory benefit that all they need to think about is being on God's side and doing work inspired by his will, whose instruments their enemies are.

The unique and infallible power of divine action always influences the simple in the right way, inwardly directing them to react wisely to everything. They welcome all that comes their way, everything that happens to them, everything they experience excepting sin. Sometimes this happens consciously; but sometimes simple souls are moved by mysterious impulses, unconsciously to say, do or ignore things, often for quite natural reasons, in which they see no mystery; things which seem like pure chance, necessity, or convenience, and seem even to have no significance either to themselves or to others. And yet divine action, in the form of intelligence, wisdom and advice of their friends, uses them all for the benefit of these souls, ingeniously foiling the plans of those who scheme to harm them. To deal with the pure heart is to deal with God.
–Jean-Pierre de Caussade

JEAN-PIERRE DE CAUSSADE
(1675-1751)

A French writer and preacher, he was among the last of the seventeenth-century mystical school. He arrived on the church historical scene just as Innocent XI was denouncing the spiritual system of Quietism, a belief that passive contemplation provides the Christian a personal union with God that overrides the need for the ordinances of the church. Caussade sought to help Christians distinguish between extreme forms of Quietism and authentic, moment-by-moment dependence on God. His writings were passed from hand to hand before being published in 1867.

# GIVING YOUR ALL

WITH EVERY NOBLE, GODLY THOUGHT THAT COMES TO YOUR MIND, WITH EVERY PROMISE YOU MAKE IN A MOMENT OF CONVICTING PRAYER, YOUR ENEMY CAN ALWAYS HELP YOU THINK OF THREE OR FOUR REASONS WHY TAKING THIS THING TOO SERIOUSLY CAN CAUSE MORE TROUBLE THAN IT'S WORTH. BUT IF YOU WANT TO LOOK BACK ON LIFE WITH FEW REGRETS, YOU KNOW WHAT YOU CAN DO WITH HIS SUGGESTIONS.

### Philippians 1:12-14, 20-21; Galatians 2:20

Now I want you to know, brothers, that what has happened to me has really served to advance the gospel. As a result, it has become clear throughout the whole palace guard and to everyone else that I am in chains for Christ.

Because of my chains, most of the brothers in the Lord have been encouraged to speak the word of God more courageously and fearlessly....

I eagerly expect and hope that I will in no way be ashamed, but will have sufficient courage so that now as always Christ will be exalted in my body, whether by life or by death. For to me, to live is Christ and to die is gain....

I have been crucified with Christ and I no longer live, but Christ lives in me. The life I live in the body, I live by faith in the Son of God, who loved me and gave himself for me.

PERSONALLY SPEAKING *You'll find that the faith and resolve you sense in quiet times of prayer are much closer to God's heart than the excuses you come up with through the day. Do what He's dreaming in you.*

# CLASSIC *Insights*

We shall all feel very much ashamed if we do not yield to Jesus on the point He has asked us to yield to Him. Paul says, "My determination is to be my utmost for His Highest." To get there is a question of will, not of debate nor of reasoning, but a surrender on that point.

An overweening consideration for ourselves is the thing that keeps us from that decision, though we put it that we are considering others. When we consider what it will cost others if we obey the call of Jesus, we tell God He does not know what our obedience will mean.

Keep to the point; He does know. Shut out every other consideration and keep yourself before God for this one thing only—My Utmost for His Highest. I am determined to be absolutely and entirely for Him and for Him alone.

"Whether that means life or death, no matter!" (v. 21). Paul is determined that nothing shall deter him from doing exactly what God wants. God's order has to work up to a crisis in our lives because we will not heed the gentler way. He brings us to the place where He asks us to be our utmost for Him, and we begin to debate; then He produces a providential crisis where we have to decide—for or against, and from that point the "Great Divide" begins. If the crisis has come to you on any line, surrender your will to Him absolutely and irrevocably.

—Oswald Chambers

OSWALD
CHAMBERS
(1874-1917)

In 1911 he founded the Bible Training College in London, which he closed in 1915 to serve as a YMCA chaplain in Egypt during World War I, but he died shortly thereafter following surgery for a ruptured appendix. He wrote only one book, but more than thirty bear his name, thanks to his wife's tireless efforts to transcribe her shorthand notes of his messages. One of these, *My Utmost for His Highest,* has been continually in print in the United States since 1935 and remains among the top ten Christian bestsellers.

# LITTLE THINGS

WHAT IF . . . INSTEAD OF LISTENING TO THE RADIO IN THE CAR, YOU SPEND SOME TIME LISTENING TO GOD? INSTEAD OF RUNNING DOWN A COWORKER BEHIND HIS BACK, YOU TAKE HIM OUT TO LUNCH AND TALK ABOUT THINGS MORE IMPORTANT THAN WORK? INSTEAD OF SIMPLY FASTING THROUGH A MEAL EACH WEEK, YOU BUY ONE FOR A HUNGRY MAN—AND TELL HIM ABOUT LIVING BREAD? LITTLE THINGS. THEY ADD UP.

## Hebrews 5:13-14; 6:1, 7-8, 11-12

*Anyone who lives on milk, being still an infant, is not acquainted with the teaching about righteousness. But solid food is for the mature, who by constant use have trained themselves to distinguish good from evil. . . . Therefore let us leave the elementary teachings about Christ and go on to maturity . . .*

*Land that drinks in the rain often falling on it and that produces a crop useful to those for whom it is farmed receives the blessing of God. But land that produces thorns and thistles is worthless and is in danger of being cursed. In the end it will be burned. . . .*

*We want each of you to show this same diligence to the very end, in order to make your hope sure. We do not want you to become lazy, but to imitate those who through faith and patience inherit what has been promised.*

PERSONALLY SPEAKING *Wanting to do greater things for God? He knows that we're not ready for the bigger things until we're faithful in the little ones. What's something little you can do for Him today?*

_____

_____

_____

_____

_____

_____

# CLASSIC *Insights*

The way to become able to do great things is to do our little things with endless repetition, and with increasing dexterity and carefulness. The way to grow into Christlikeness of character, is to watch ourselves in the minutest things of thought and word and act, until our powers are trained to go almost without watching in the lines of moral right and holy beauty.

To become prayerful, we must learn to pray by the clock, at fixed times. It is fine ideal talk to say that our devotions should be like the bird's song, warbling out anywhere and at any time with sweet unrestraint; but in plain truth, to depend upon such impulses as guides to praying, would soon lead to no praying at all. This may do for heavenly life; but we have not gotten into heaven yet, and until we do, we need to pray by habit. So of all religious life.

We only grow into patience by being as patient as we can, daily and hourly, and in smallest matters, ever learning to be more and more patient until we reach the highest possible culture in that line. We can only become unselfish wherever we have an opportunity, until our life grows into the permanent beauty of unselfishness. We can only grow better by striving ever to be better than we already are, and by climbing step by step toward the radiant heights of excellence.

–J. Wilbur Chapman

J. WILBUR CHAPMAN (1859-1918)

Born in Richmond, Indiana, this Presbyterian preacher known for his calm, yet forceful oratory was ordained in 1882 and held pastorates in several states before devoting more than half of his lifetime ministry to evangelism. Along the way, he joined forces with the greats of early 20th-century revivalists, including D. L. Moody, R. A. Torrey, and C. M. Alexander. He also became director of the Winona Lake Bible Conference and was instrumental in winning thousands of souls to Christ around the world.

# MYSTERY OF HIS MIGHT

SCIENTISTS WHO ONCE THOUGHT THE UNIVERSE WAS SLOWLY COLLAPSING IN ON ITSELF ARE NOW DISCOVERING THAT IT'S INSTEAD GETTING BIGGER. SOMEHOW, THEY SAY, A CREATIVE FORCE IS COUNTERING THE NATURAL EFFECTS OF GRAVITY BY IMPLEMENTING A FORM OF ANTIGRAVITATIONAL POWER. THEY DON'T KNOW WHAT IT IS YET. NO BIG BANG-UP THEORY HAS EMERGED FROM THE RESEARCH. CAN YOU THINK OF ANYTHING?

## Daniel 6:19-22a, 25-27

*At the first light of dawn, the king got up and hurried to the lions' den. When he came near the den, he called to Daniel in an anguished voice, "Daniel, servant of the living God, has your God, whom you serve continually, been able to rescue you from the lions?"*

*Daniel answered, "O king, live forever! My God sent his angel, and he shut the mouths of the lions. They have not hurt me. . . ."*

*Then King Darius wrote to all the peoples, nations and men of every language throughout the land: "May you prosper greatly! I issue a decree that in every part of my kingdom people must fear and reverence the God of Daniel. For he is the living God and he endures forever; his kingdom will not be destroyed, his dominion will never end. He rescues and he saves; he performs signs and wonders in the heavens and on the earth. He has rescued Daniel from the power of the lions."*

PERSONALLY SPEAKING *Isn't it great to know that the God who conceived the world in His own mind and keeps it floating through space without a bobble considers us one of His kids? Now that's a mystery.*

And so she floated many a year and day, Across the Aegean sea, into the Strait

Of Gibraltar, as fortune would direct. Many a scant and meagre meal she ate,

Many a time she thought that she must die, Before the weltering waves would cast her up

To land her at the place ordained by fate.

You may well ask me why she was not slain With others at the feast? Who was there to save?

To that demand this answer I return: Who rescued Daniel from the fearsome den

Where everyone but he, master and man, Was eaten by the lion, nor might escape?

No one but God, whom he bore in his heart.

God chose to show His miraculous power through her, that we might see His mighty works;

And Christ, the remedy for every sorrow, As learned men know, chooses His instruments

For purposes that are obscure and dark to human wit, because our ignorance

Can never wholly grasp His providence.

–Geoffrey Chaucer

GEOFFREY CHAUCER
(1343-1400)

Chaucer played many roles in his life: soldier, diplomat, intelligence officer, construction supervisor, Controller of Customs, member of Parliament, living in a turbulent England witnessing the seeds of individualism sprouting through Wycliffe and his followers. He began work on *The Canterbury Tales* about 1387, intending for each of his thirty pilgrims to tell four stories each. Though unfinished at his death, it received instant acclaim for its accurate, vivid portrayal of human nature.

# NATURAL DELIGHT

INSIDE, THE TV WAS BLARING SOMETHING ABOUT LAB RATS GETTING SICK FROM TOMATO JUICE; ONE OF THE KIDS WAS COMING IN CRYING WITH AN UGLY SCRAPE ON HER KNEE. THE BEANS WERE BOILING OVER, AND THE SALAD HADN'T BEEN MADE. BUT OUTSIDE, BLUE SKIES WERE BECOMING SPRINKLED WITH RED AND PURPLE, THE SUN SINKING IN A SPECTACULAR SPLASH OF AWE AND GLORY. DIDN'T YOU NOTICE?

## Psalm 104:24-31

How many are your works, O LORD! In wisdom you made them all; the earth is full of your creatures.

There is the sea, vast and spacious, teeming with creatures beyond number–living things both large and small. There the ships go to and fro, and the leviathan, which you formed to frolic there.

These all look to you to give them their food at the proper time. When you give it to them, they gather it up; when you open your hand, they are satisfied with good things.

When you hide your face, they are terrified; when you take away their breath, they die and return to the dust. When you send your Spirit, they are created, and you renew the face of the earth.

May the glory of the LORD endure forever; may the LORD rejoice in his works–he who looks at the earth, and it trembles, who touches the mountains, and they smoke.

PERSONALLY SPEAKING *Something goes out of life when we just get too plain busy to enjoy God's simple things. Next time you get a chance, listen for the katydids or watch a spider build a web. God does.*

Now, to put the matter in a popular phrase, it might be true that the sun rises regularly because he never gets tired of rising. His routine might be due, not to a lifelessness, but to a rush of life.

The thing I mean can be seen, for instance, in children, when they find some game or joke that they specially enjoy.... Because children have abounding vitality, because they are in spirit fierce and free, therefore they want things repeated and unchanged. They always say, "Do it again"; and the grown-up person does it again until he is nearly dead. For grown-up people are not strong enough to exult in monotony. But perhaps God is strong enough to exult in monotony. It is possible that God says every morning, "Do it again" to the sun; and every evening, "Do it again" to the moon.

It may not be automatic necessity that makes all daisies alike; it may be that God makes every daisy separately, but has never gotten tired of making them. It may be that He has the eternal appetite of infancy; for we have sinned and grown old, and our Father is younger than we. The repetition in Nature may not be a mere recurrence; it may be a theatrical encore.

–G. K. Chesterton

G. K.
CHESTERTON
(1874-1936)

He was one of the most prolific, versatile writers of all time, known for his witty, sarcastic, almost brutal honesty and observations. He was the author of over one hundred books and a contributor to two hundred more, on everything from Christian apologetics to his Father Brown detective series, as well as an ongoing journalist.

A large man of stature, he was as prophetic as he was profound, foreseeing such historical developments as the rise and fall of Nazism and Communism and the cultural chaos of modernism.

# SOMEONE'S WATCHING

AT A CERTAIN AGE, YOU CAN GET INTO AN R-RATED MOVIE WITHOUT A SECOND LOOK FROM THE TICKET TAKER. IN FACT, WITHIN LEGAL LIMITS, YOU CAN DO JUST ABOUT ANYTHING YOU WANT WITH YOUR FREE TIME. BUT JUST BECAUSE YOU CAN DO SOMETHING DOESN'T MEAN IT'S THE RIGHT THING TO DO, WHETHER YOUR FRIENDS UNDERSTAND YOUR REASONS OR NOT. YOU'RE SETTING AN EXAMPLE. ISN'T THAT GOOD ENOUGH?

## Psalm 71:14-18; Romans 14:17, 21-22

But as for me, I will always have hope; I will praise you more and more. My mouth will tell of your righteousness, of your salvation all day long, though I know not its measure. I will come and proclaim your mighty acts, O Sovereign LORD; I will proclaim your righteousness, yours alone.

Since my youth, O God, you have taught me, and to this day I declare your marvelous deeds. Even when I am old and gray, do not forsake me, O God, till I declare your power to the next generation, your might to all who are to come. . . .

For the kingdom of God is not a matter of eating and drinking, but of righteousness, peace and joy in the Holy Spirit. . . . It is better not to eat meat or drink wine or to do anything else that will cause your brother to fall. So whatever you believe about these things keep between yourself and God. Blessed is the man who does not condemn himself by what he approves.

PERSONALLY SPEAKING *Take a discerning look at your own recreational habits. What do they say to your family, your children, your unsaved neighbors? Are you being a little too free with your own free time?*

_____

_____

_____

_____

_____

_____

# CLASSIC *Insights*

Again there are chariot races and satanic spectacles in the hippodrome, and our congregation is shrinking. They have cast altogether out of their minds the memory of the holy season of Lent, the feast of salvation on the day of the Resurrection, their awesome and ineffable communion in the divine mysteries, and my series of instructions.

Not only will they receive the serious injury that comes from such negligence, but they will also be the occasion for scandal to others. Who, then, will pardon them? Who will pardon the old man who takes no thought of his age, nor of the proximity of death, nor the enormous burden of his past sins, but each day multiplies his offenses and becomes for the young their teacher in the ways of laxity? When, tell me, will such a man be able to correct the laxity of his son or control the young man of disordered passions, when he himself has not learned self-control at his time of life?

The man who pursues virtue not only expects recompense in return for his toils, but also reaps a reward for the help he has given to others by leading them to a zeal for and imitation of his own virtue. In the same way, those who pursue wickedness render a more severe account, because they provide others with an occasion for being lax. How, then, shall I admonish the young, when those who have grown old have fallen into such laxity and heed not the exhortation of the Apostle, who said: "Do not be a stumbling block to Jews and Greeks and to the Church of God"?

–John Chrysostom

JOHN CHRYSOSTOM (344-407)

He preached with such straightforwardness and integrity in the cathedral at Antioch, he was tagged with the name *chrysostomos* ("golden-mouthed"). But his preaching suffered a fatal blow after he was appointed bishop of Constantinople. His uncompromising zeal and political naiveté offended Empress Eudoxia and the surrounding clergy, who contrived charges of heresy against him and had him deposed. After returning only to infuriate the empress a second time, he was again exiled, but died on the journey.

# SERIOUS SCRIPTURE

IF YOU'VE EVER TRIED LIVING THROUGH A TOUGH DECISION WITHOUT EXERCISING THE PRIVILEGE OF READING GOD'S WORD EVERY DAY, YOU KNOW WHAT IT'S LIKE TO HAVE YOUR THOUGHTS WHIPPED INTO EVERY DIRECTION, YOUR DISCERNMENT JAMMED BY CONFLICTING SIGNALS, YOUR EMOTIONS TORN IN TWO. OUR OWN INSTINCTS CAN'T REALLY TELL US MUCH WHEN THEY'RE NOT IN TUNE WITH THE TRUTH.

## *Psalm 19:7-11; 119:92-93, 103-104*

*The law of the LORD is perfect, reviving the soul. The statutes of the LORD are trustworthy, making wise the simple.*

*The precepts of the LORD are right, giving joy to the heart. The commands of the LORD are radiant, giving light to the eyes.*

*The fear of the LORD is pure, enduring forever. The ordinances of the LORD are sure and altogether righteous. They are more precious than gold, than much pure gold; they are sweeter than honey, than honey from the comb. By them is your servant warned; in keeping them there is great reward. . . .*

*If your law had not been my delight, I would have perished in my affliction. I will never forget your precepts, for by them you have preserved my life. . . .*

*How sweet are your words to my taste, sweeter than honey to my mouth! I gain understanding from your precepts; therefore I hate every wrong path.*

PERSONALLY SPEAKING *No Bible, no breakfast. That's a pretty good motto to remember when everything else seems more important than a daily dunk in God's eternal Word. Don't ever leave home without it.*

_____

_____

_____

_____

_____

_____

To those who seriously ask the question, How may we profit most, and grow wise unto salvation, by reading the sacred writings? I answer:

1. Deeply consider that it is your duty and interest to read the Holy Scriptures.

2. When you read, consider that it is God's Word which you read; and that his faithfulness is pledged to fulfill both its promises and threatenings.

3. Read the whole Bible, and read it in order; two chapters in the Old Testament and one in the New, daily if you can possibly spare the time; and you will have more time than you are aware of; if you retrench all needless visits, and save the hours spent in useless or unimportant conversation.

4. Think that the eye of God is upon you while you are reading his Word: and read and hear it with that reverence with which you would hear God speak, were he to address you as he did the prophets and people of old; for, be assured, that he considers it as much his Word now as he did when he first spoke it.

–Adam Clarke

ADAM CLARKE
(1762-1832)

This Methodist theologian got his first taste for religious instruction under John Wesley's influence at the Kingswood School in London. He was appointed as a circuit preacher in Wiltshire in 1782, but as his fame grew, he traveled extensively throughout the British Isles. Three times he was president of the Methodist conference and continued to excel in scholarship on a wide range of disciplines. His crowning literary achievement was an eight-volume commentary comprising over sixteen years of study.

# JUST WAIT AND SEE

YOU MAY NOT BE ABLE TO SATISFACTORILY PROVE TO YOUR CHILDREN THAT EVERYTHING YOU'RE TEACHING THEM IS THE ABSOLUTE TRUTH—THAT GOD'S WAY IS ALWAYS BEST, AND THAT TRUSTING HIM IS THE ONLY SURE COURSE IN LIFE. BUT THOSE WHO SIMPLY MUST FIND THINGS OUT FOR THEMSELVES WILL FIND OUT SOON ENOUGH. PRAY THAT THOSE WITHIN YOUR REACH WON'T CHOOSE TO LEARN THE HARD WAY.

## Deuteronomy 32:10-12, 15-18

*In a desert land he found him, in a barren and howling waste. He shielded him and cared for him; he guarded him as the apple of his eye, like an eagle that stirs up its nest and hovers over its young, that spreads its wings to catch them and carries them on its pinions. The LORD alone led him; no foreign god was with him. . . .*

*Jeshurun grew fat and kicked; filled with food, he became heavy and sleek. He abandoned the God who made him and rejected the Rock his Savior.*

*They made him jealous with their foreign gods and angered him with their detestable idols. They sacrificed to demons, which are not God—gods they had not known, gods that recently appeared, gods your fathers did not fear.*

*You deserted the Rock, who fathered you; you forgot the God who gave you birth.*

PERSONALLY SPEAKING *You can talk and talk till you're blue in the face, but the best way to prepare your children for a faithful future is to stay in God's ear about it. He's the one who'll be going out there with them.*

# CLASSIC *Insights*

The all-merciful and beneficent Father has bowels [of compassion] towards those that fear Him, and kindly and lovingly bestows His favors upon those who come to Him with a simple mind. Wherefore let us not be double-minded; neither let our soul be lifted up on account of His exceedingly great and glorious gifts.

Far from us be that which is written, "Wretched are they who are of a double mind, and of a doubting heart; who say, These things we have heard even in the times of our fathers; but, behold, we have grown old, and none of them has happened unto us."

You foolish ones! Compare yourselves to a tree: take [for instance] the vine. First of all, it sheds its leaves, then it buds, next it puts forth leaves, and then it flowers; after that comes the sour grape, and then follows the ripened fruit. Ye perceive how in a little time the fruit of a tree comes to maturity. Of a truth, soon and suddenly shall His will be accomplished, as the Scripture also bears witness, saying, "Speedily will He come, and will not tarry"; and, "The Lord shall suddenly come to His temple, even the Holy One, for whom ye look."
–Clement of Rome

CLEMENT OF ROME (FIRST CENTURY A.D.)

Clement was the fourth bishop of Rome and perhaps the "Clement" mentioned in Philippians 4:3. His letter to the Corinthians is his best-known writing, penned around a.d. 96 and included in an early version of the New Testament, though never universally accepted as inspired. Tradition has it that he was exiled under the emperor Domitian (like the Apostle John) and forced into hard labor in the mines, continuing to win converts until he was hurled into the sea with an anchor around his neck. The anchor remains his symbol.

# Getting Over Getting Even

Only you know how hard a problem revenge is for you. Maybe revenge is too strong a word. Maybe you've just got one of those brothers-in-law who gets under your skin something awful, who thinks his way is the only way, and makes little joking remarks about your religion. You don't want to hurt him or anything. But how far would you go to help him?

## 1 Samuel 26:7-11a; Romans 12:20-21

So David and Abishai went to the army by night, and there was Saul, lying asleep inside the camp with his spear stuck in the ground near his head. Abner and the soldiers were lying around him. Abishai said to David, "Today God has delivered your enemy into your hands. Now let me pin him to the ground with one thrust of my spear; I won't strike him twice."

But David said to Abishai, "Don't destroy him! Who can lay a hand on the Lord's anointed and be guiltless? As surely as the Lord lives," he said, "the Lord himself will strike him; either his time will come and he will die, or he will go into battle and perish. But the Lord forbid that I should lay a hand on the Lord's anointed. . . ."

On the contrary: "If your enemy is hungry, feed him; if he is thirsty, give him something to drink. In doing this, you will heap burning coals on his head."

Do not be overcome by evil, but overcome evil with good.

PERSONALLY SPEAKING *Is there someone in your life right now that you'd consider an enemy? Someone who enjoys making you feel uncomfortable? Working for his or her good isn't a comfortable option. But it is God's.*

Since I know, beloved brethren, that very many are eager, either on account of the burden or the pain of smarting wrongs, to be quickly avenged of those who act harshly and rage against them, we must not withhold the fact that placed as we are in the midst of these storms of a jarring world, we may patiently wait for the day of God's vengeance, and not hurry to revenge our suffering with a querulous haste. The Lord commands us to wait, and to bear with brave patience the day of future vengeance. . . .

Let us wait for Him, beloved brethren, our Judge and Avenger, who shall equally avenge with Himself the congregation of His Church, and the number of all the righteous from the beginning of the world. Let him who hurries, and is too impatient for his revenge, consider that even He Himself is not yet avenged who is the Avenger. How great is His patience, that He who is adored in heaven is not yet avenged on earth! Let us, beloved brethren, consider His patience in our persecutions and sufferings; let us give an obedience full of expectation to His advent; and let us not hasten, servants as we are, to be defended before our Lord with irreligious and immodest eagerness. Let us rather press onward and labor, and watching with our whole heart, and steadfast to all endurance, let us keep the Lord's precepts; so that when the day of anger and vengeance shall come, we may not be judged with the impious and sinners, but may be honored with the righteous and those that fear God.

–Cyprian of Carthage

CYPRIAN OF
CARTHAGE
(200-258)

Cyprian wasn't even converted until he was in his forties, but his full and immediate dedication to Christian faith, morals, and practice, along with his native ability in leadership, caused a meteoric rise into the bishopric of Carthage. His controversial views on water baptism and the laying on of hands drew a threat of excommunication from Rome, though the death of Stephen I and a new wave of persecution delayed his demise for another year. He was finally banished to Curubis and beheaded outside Carthage.

# GUARD ON DUTY

CONSCIENCE IS A SIGN THAT GOD'S INSIDE. THAT NAGGING PAIN THAT MAKES YOU WALK PAST THE DROP BOX AT THE LIBRARY AND GO INSIDE TO PAY YOUR OVERDUE FINES, THAT'S GOD. THAT UNSETTLING FEELING THAT CATCHES IN YOUR THROAT WHEN YOU'RE UNDERCHARGED AT THE BURGER PLACE, THAT'S GOD. AND THAT'S GOOD. BECAUSE KNOWING THAT SIN STILL MAKES YOU SICK IS A SURE SIGN OF GOOD HEALTH.

## 1 John 2:3-6; 3:21-24

We know that we have come to know him if we obey his commands.

The man who says, "I know him," but does not do what he commands is a liar, and the truth is not in him. But if anyone obeys his word, God's love is truly made complete in him.

This is how we know we are in him: Whoever claims to live in him must walk as Jesus did. . . .

Dear friends, if our hearts do not condemn us, we have confidence before God and receive from him anything we ask, because we obey his commands and do what pleases him.

And this is his command: to believe in the name of his Son, Jesus Christ, and to love one another as he commanded us.

Those who obey his commands live in him, and he in them. And this is how we know that he lives in us: We know it by the Spirit he gave us.

PERSONALLY SPEAKING *God deserves a great big thank-you today for being willing to risk your happiness in order to preserve your holiness. Conscience is a gift only a true, loving Father would give.*

The notion of moral government and the feeling of its necessity springs up naturally in the human mind; but no earthly form of it satisfies our desires or meets our necessities.

Conscience restrains us, and when we have disregarded its monitions, stings us with remorse; but men are still wicked. Public sentiment stamps vice with infamy; but in spite of public sentiment, men are vicious. Civil government holds out its penalties, and the ruler brandishes his sword; but men persevere in wickedness, and often with impunity.

The voice of nature within us calls for a government free from these imperfections. If, from the idea of a petty ruler over a single tribe or nation we ascend to that of a moral governor over all intelligent creatures; if instead of the imperfect moral judgments and feelings which we find in men, we attribute to this universal ruler all possible moral perfections; if we invest him with knowledge sufficient to detect every crime, and power sufficient to manifest his disapprobation of it in the most suitable and effectual way; and if this exalted sovereign, instead of being far from us, is brought into such a relation to us that in him we live, move, and have our being, we shall have the most sublime conception of moral government of which our minds are capable.

–J. L. Dagg

J. L. DAGG
(1794-1884)

His was not a gentle ride into success and acclaim. A freak injury at twenty-five years of age placed him on crutches the rest of his life. At thirty, he nearly lost his eyesight. And at forty, another affliction destroyed his voice, making it impossible for him to speak without great pain. Yet at fifty, he assumed the presidency of Mercer University in Macon, Georgia, and enjoyed a tenure of productive peace that earned him a renowned reputation as a silent scholar whose wisdom and steadiness had been forged in the fire.

# THE GOD WHO IS NEAR

IT'S ONE THING TO KNOW THE NAME OF THE FRIEND WHO GOES TO CHURCH WITH YOUR SEC-OND COUSIN, WHO KNOWS SOMEONE WHO WORKS FOR A PROFESSIONAL BALL TEAM. IT'S QUITE ANOTHER FOR HIM TO CALL YOU UP ON THE PHONE ONE DAY TO TELL YOU HE'S GOT FOUR TICK-ETS FOR NEXT SATURDAY'S GAME . . . IF YOU WANT THEM. IT'S NOT WHO YOU KNOW. IT'S WHO TAKES TIME TO KNOW YOU THAT REALLY MATTERS.

## *Hebrews 2:11, 17; 4:14-16*

Both the one who makes men holy and those who are made holy are of the same family. So Jesus is not ashamed to call them brothers. . . .

For this reason he had to be made like his brothers in every way, in order that he might become a merciful and faithful high priest in service to God, and that he might make atonement for the sins of the people. . . .

Therefore, since we have a great high priest who has gone through the heavens, Jesus the Son of God, let us hold firmly to the faith we profess.

For we do not have a high priest who is unable to sympathize with our weaknesses, but we have one who has been tempted in every way, just as we are–yet was without sin.

Let us then approach the throne of grace with confidence, so that we may receive mercy and find grace to help us in our time of need.

PERSONALLY SPEAKING *When's the last time you took five minutes to consider the things Christ gave up to come down where we are? He must really love us. And He must really like to hear us love Him back.*

There are times, I suppose, in the history of many of us when, though we hardly acknowledge it to ourselves, there is a latent discontent that He who created the world should, as we imagine, have no share in its troubles.

The Christian doctrine of the Trinity meets these cravings, and more than meets them. Christ not only reveals the Infinite and the Eternal God who in His Infinitude and Eternity transcends the universe and remains forever above and apart from it. He accepts human limitations, knows (by actual experience) human joys and the sharpest of human pains; He hungers and thirsts; He has not where to lay His head; He has friends who love Him and whom He loves; He has bitter enemies; He is tempted; He dies a cruel death. . . .

This is a most wonderful and glorious revelation of God. It is true that God transcends the universe and that the distance between Him and our race is infinite. But it is also true that in the Eternal life of the Godhead there is a divine Person so near akin to us that it was possible for Him to take our life into His own, to "become flesh," to make His home in the world, to share the happiness and the misery of the race. Now we know that God is a God "nigh at hand" as well as a God "afar off."

–R. W. Dale

R. W. DALE
(1829-1895)

Dale graduated in London with a degree in philosophy and began his career as a schoolmaster, but soon turned to the ministry, becoming pastor in 1853 at Carr's Lane Chapel in Birmingham. From this position, he wielded considerable influence in the political and social life of the city, espousing liberal views on government and education, and joining in every controversy of the day. His most famous work was *The Atonement,* which he expressed in ethical and moral terms, as well as in legal ones.

# FULL FORGIVENESS

YOU MIGHT CALL IT THE DOCTRINE OF LAST THINGS—THE SUPERSTITIOUS NOTION THAT A PER-
SON'S ETERNAL DESTINY IS SOLELY DETERMINED BY WHAT HE'S DOING AT THE MOMENT OF
DEATH—AS IF GOD'S GRACE IS SO CHEAP THAT A SIN COULD SNEAK IN UNDER THE WIRE AND
NEGATE THE PRICE OF HIS REDEMPTION. SURE, SIN IS SERIOUS BUSINESS. BUT FOR THE
CHRISTIAN, THE METER QUIT RUNNING A LONG TIME AGO.

## 1 John 2:1-2; Hebrews 7:25-28

*My dear children, I write this to you so that you will not sin. But
if anybody does sin, we have one who speaks to the Father in our
defense–Jesus Christ, the Righteous One. He is the atoning sacrifice
for our sins, and not only for ours but also for the sins of the whole
world. . . .*

*Therefore he is able to save completely those who come to God
through him, because he always lives to intercede for them.*

*Such a high priest meets our need–one who is holy, blameless,
pure, set apart from sinners, exalted above the heavens.*

*Unlike the other high priests, he does not need to offer sacrifices
day after day, first for his own sins, and then for the sins of the people. He sacrificed for their sins once for all when he offered himself.*

*For the law appoints as high priests men who are weak; but the
oath, which came after the law, appointed the Son, who has been
made perfect forever.*

PERSONALLY SPEAKING *Have you gotten tripped up by an old familiar habit
again? Confess it to get your heart right, repent to get yourself back on track, but
forget about God calling you on it later.*

Christ died for sins once for all, and the man who believes in Christ and in His death has his relation to God once for all determined not by sin but by the Atonement.

The sin for which a Christian has daily to seek forgiveness is not sin which annuls his acceptance with God, and casts him back into the position of one who has never had the assurance of the pardoning mercy of God in Christ; on the contrary, that assurance ought to be the permanent element in his life. The forgiveness of sins has to be received again and again as sin emerges into act; but when the soul closes with Christ the propitiation, the assurance of God's love is laid at the foundation of its being once for all. It is not to isolated acts it refers, but to the personality; not to sins, but to the sinner; not to the past only, in which wrong has been done, but to time and eternity.

There will inevitably be in the Christian life experiences of sinning and being forgiven, of falling and being restored. But the grace which forgives and restores is not some new thing, nor is it conditioned in some new way. It is not dependent upon penitence, or works, or merit of ours; it is the same absolutely free grace which meets us at the Cross. From first to last, it is the blood of Jesus, God's Son, which cleanses from sin.

–James Denney

JAMES DENNEY
(1856-1917)

Denney published a series of commentaries during his eleven years of ministry at the East Church, Broughty Ferry, Scotland, before returning to academic life at his alma mater—the Free Church College in Glasgow. He was a strong advocate of temperance and civic righteousness, as well as an outspoken leader in what came to be known as the United Free Church of Scotland. He continued his work, though, to bring unity among all the churches of his nation, and left behind many literary volumes.

# TWO SIDES OF TROUBLE

AND SO, AS THE STORY GOES, WHEN THE SHEPHERD FOUND THE STRAGGLING SHEEP HAD WAN-
DERED OFF INTO HARM'S WAY AGAIN, HE DELIBERATELY BROKE ONE OF ITS LEGS, ENSURING THAT
THE WORDS OF WARNING THE SHEEP HAD FAILED TO HEAR WITH ITS EARS WOULD NOW BE FELT
IN ITS BONES. AND BY HAVING TO BE CARRIED A WHILE, IT WOULD LEARN THAT THE HANDS
THAT DISCIPLINE ARE ALSO THE HANDS THAT PROTECT.

## Job 5:17-18; 33:19-22, 25-28

"Blessed is the man whom God corrects; so do not despise the discipline of the Almighty. For he wounds, but he also binds up; he
injures, but his hands also heal. . . ."

"Or a man may be chastened on a bed of pain with constant distress in his bones, so that his very being finds food repulsive and his
soul loathes the choicest meal. His flesh wastes away to nothing, and
his bones, once hidden, now stick out. His soul draws near to the pit,
and his life to the messengers of death. . . ."

"Then his flesh is renewed like a child's; it is restored as in the
days of his youth. He prays to God and finds favor with him, he sees
God's face and shouts for joy; he is restored by God to his righteous
state.

"Then he comes to men and says, 'I sinned, and perverted what
was right, but I did not get what I deserved. He redeemed my soul
from going down to the pit, and I will live to enjoy the light.'"

PERSONALLY SPEAKING *The problem you're facing right now may not be a
direct act of God's discipline. But it certainly won't hurt to act like it is and to
make sure God's got you right where He can use you.*

---

---

---

---

---

---

O eternal and most gracious God, who gave manna to your servants in the wilderness, bread so conditioned, qualified so, as that to every man manna tasted like that which that man liked best, I humbly beseech you to make this correction, which I acknowledge to be part of my daily bread–that it would taste so to me, not as I would but as you would have it taste, and to conform my taste, and make it agreeable to your will.

You would have your corrections taste of humiliation, but you would have them taste of consolation too; taste of danger, but taste of assurance too.

As therefore you have imprinted two manifest qualities in all the elements of which our bodies consist, so that as your fire dries, so it heats too; and as your water moists, so it cools too; so, O Lord, in these corrections which are the elements of our regeneration, by which our souls are made yours, imprint your two qualities, those two operations, that, as they scourge us, they may scourge us into the way to you; that when they have showed us that we are nothing in ourselves, they may also show us, that you are all things unto us.

–John Donne

**JOHN DONNE**
(1573-1631)

After stints at both Oxford and Cambridge, he found work with the lord chancellor, Sir Thomas Egerton, but enraged him by eloping with his niece and was jailed. After his release he took to writing poems, but after fourteen years of coaxing by friends and family, he became a minister in the Church of England and eventually dean of St. Paul's. Yet he is best remembered for his poetry, a rare mix of passionate sonnets and dark, heavy sermons, such as *For Whom the Bell Tolls*—"it tolls for thee."

# I Promise You This

SOMEWHERE IN YOUR NOTES AND PAPERS IS PROBABLY A LIST FROM LAST NEW YEAR'S—RESOLUTIONS THAT LOOKED REALLY NICE WHEN YOU WROTE THEM OUT IN LONGHAND, BUT . . . WELL . . . LET'S JUST SAY YOU'VE COME UP A LITTLE SHORT. WHAT NOW, THEN? PROMISE NEVER TO MAKE PROMISES LIKE THAT AGAIN? OR TO MAKE YOURSELF LOOK STRAIGHT INTO THE EYES OF UNKEPT PROMISES AND DARE TO MAKE THEM AGAIN?

## Joshua 24:14-15, 25-27

"Now fear the LORD and serve him with all faithfulness. Throw away the gods your forefathers worshiped beyond the River and in Egypt, and serve the LORD.

"But if serving the LORD seems undesirable to you, then choose for yourselves this day whom you will serve, whether the gods your forefathers served beyond the River, or the gods of the Amorites, in whose land you are living. But as for me and my household, we will serve the LORD." . . .

On that day Joshua made a covenant for the people, and there at Shechem he drew up for them decrees and laws. And Joshua recorded these things in the Book of the Law of God. Then he took a large stone and set it up there under the oak near the holy place of the LORD.

"See!" he said to all the people. "This stone will be a witness against us. It has heard all the words the LORD has said to us. It will be a witness against you if you are untrue to your God."

PERSONALLY SPEAKING   *If it's been a while, how about making an appointment with yourself this week to make a fresh list of resolutions? Don't get discouraged. There's never a bad time to make a fresh start.*

_____

_____

_____

_____

_____

_____

1. Resolved, that I will do whatsoever I think to be most to God's glory, and my own good, profit and pleasure, in the whole of my duration, without any consideration of the time, whether now, or never so many myriads of ages hence. Resolved to do whatever I think to be my duty and most for the good and advantage of mankind in general. Resolved to do this, whatever difficulties I meet with, how many soever, and how great soever.

2. Resolved, to be continually endeavoring to find out some new contrivance and invention to promote the aforementioned things.

3. Resolved, if ever I shall fall and grow dull, so as to neglect to keep any part of these Resolutions, to repent of all I can remember, when I come to myself again.

4. Resolved, never to do any manner of thing, whether in soul or body, less or more, but what tends to the glory of God; nor be, nor suffer it, if I can avoid it.

5. Resolved, never to lose one moment of time, but improve it the most profitable way I possibly can.

6. Resolved, to live with all my might, while I do live.

–Jonathan Edwards

JONATHAN
EDWARDS
(1703-1758)

Edwards entered Yale at thirteen, already with a firm grasp of Latin, Greek, and Hebrew. Then at twenty-one, he assumed the pastorate in Northampton, Massachusetts, where he was used of God to ignite the Great Awakening of 1734-35 and subsequent, more extensive revivals. In 1750, however, he had a falling out with his congregation over the admission of the unconverted to Communion. After years of devoting himself to frontier missions, he reluctantly accepted the presidency of Princeton in 1758, but died a month later.

_____

_____

_____

_____

_____

_____

# ALL THE RIGHT REASONS

THE PSALMIST OFTEN CALLS THEM THE "REINS"—THE PART GOD LOOKS AT WHEN HE'S INSPECTING HIS PEOPLE. ACTIONS ARE IMPORTANT. THEY TELL A LITTLE BIT ABOUT YOU. BUT THE HEART THAT HIDES BEHIND THEM, THE AMOUNT OF PRESSURE HE HAS TO APPLY TO GET YOU GOING WHERE HE WANTS—THAT'S WHAT TELLS HIM WHAT HE REALLY NEEDS TO KNOW. WHO'S BEEN PULLING YOUR REINS LATELY?

### Philippians 3:4b-11

*If anyone else thinks he has reasons to put confidence in the flesh, I have more: circumcised on the eighth day, of the people of Israel, of the tribe of Benjamin, a Hebrew of Hebrews; in regard to the law, a Pharisee; as for zeal, persecuting the church; as for legalistic righteousness, faultless.*

*But whatever was to my profit I now consider loss for the sake of Christ. What is more, I consider everything a loss compared to the surpassing greatness of knowing Christ Jesus my Lord, for whose sake I have lost all things. I consider them rubbish, that I may gain Christ and be found in him, not having a righteousness of my own that comes from the law, but that which is through faith in Christ–the righteousness that comes from God and is by faith.*

*I want to know Christ and the power of his resurrection and the fellowship of sharing in his sufferings, becoming like him in his death, and so, somehow, to attain to the resurrection from the dead.*

PERSONALLY SPEAKING *To know the heart of God, to have the mind of Christ, to respond to the gentle nudging of the Spirit, is to have the best this life has to offer. Test your motives. And give God the reins.*

# CLASSIC *Insights*

Set Christ before you as the only goal of your whole life and direct all your efforts, all your activities, all your leisure, all your business in his direction. Think of Christ, not as an empty word, but as nothing other than love, candor, patience, purity–in brief, whatever He taught. Think of the Devil as nothing but whatever things call us away from those qualities. A man impelled toward virtue alone is turning toward Christ; a man serving his own vices is surrendering to Satan. Let your eye be clear, therefore, and your whole being will be full of light. Look at Christ alone as the absolute Good, so that you may love nothing, marvel at nothing, want nothing but Christ or because of Christ; and hate nothing, despise nothing, shun nothing except wickedness or because of wickedness.

Thus it will come about that whatever you do, whether you are asleep or awake, eating or drinking, even in your very sports and pastimes . . . all of these things will be translated for you into a mountain of rewards. But if your eye is going to be misdirected and look elsewhere than at Christ, then, even if you have acted with propriety, your deeds will be barren or even injurious. For it is a fault to do even a good deed for the wrong reason.

–Erasmus

ERASMUS
(1466-1536)

He spent his most productive years in the Swiss town of Basel, where he became the first best-selling author in history. His desire was to reform the church through scholarship and instruction, to raise learning to new levels so that the rich and poor, the learned and simple, could discover spiritual life in biblical truth. In his emphasis on the use of reason, he was a forerunner of the eighteenth-century Enlightenment, yet was one of the earliest forces behind the Reformation with his emphasis on the original texts and the teachings of Christ.

# THE HIGH COST OF SIN

WONDER HOW LONG WE'LL HAVE TO LIVE BEFORE WE UNDERSTAND THAT GOD'S PROBLEM WITH SIN IS NOT WHAT IT DOES TO HIM, BUT WHAT IT DOES TO US? HE'S NOT AS ANGRY THAT WE'VE REBELLED AGAINST HIS WORD AS HE IS HURT THAT WE'VE SOLD OURSELVES TOO CHEAPLY. THOSE AREN'T LIGHTNING BOLTS IN HIS HAND. THOSE ARE TEARS IN HIS EYES THAT WE'RE MISSING THE POINT WHEN WE MISS THE MARK.

## *John 3:16-17; Romans 5:6-10*

*For God so loved the world that he gave his one and only Son, that whoever believes in him shall not perish but have eternal life. For God did not send his Son into the world to condemn the world, but to save the world through him. . . .*

*You see, at just the right time, when we were still powerless, Christ died for the ungodly.*

*Very rarely will anyone die for a righteous man, though for a good man someone might possibly dare to die. But God demonstrates his own love for us in this: While we were still sinners, Christ died for us.*

*Since we have now been justified by his blood, how much more shall we be saved from God's wrath through him! For if, when we were God's enemies, we were reconciled to him through the death of his Son, how much more, having been reconciled, shall we be saved through his life!*

PERSONALLY SPEAKING *Oh, stop and think about it. How foolish to find some sort of pleasure and entertainment in the very things that nailed Him to the cross. Turn away from your sins. The price is too high.*

Sin is the most expensive thing in the universe. Are you well aware, O sinner, what a price has been paid for you that you may be redeemed and made an heir of God and of heaven? O what an expensive business for you to indulge in sin!

Think how much machinery is kept in motion to save sinners! The Son of God was sent down–angels are sent as ministering spirits to the heirs of salvation; missionaries are sent, Christians labor, and pray, and weep in deep and anxious solicitude–all to seek and save the lost. What a wonderful, enormous tax is levied upon the benevolence of the universe to put away sin and to save the sinner! If the cost could be computed in solid gold, what a world of it–a solid globe of itself! What an array of toil and cost, from angels, Jesus Christ, the Divine Spirit, and living men!

You are right in saying that you have cost Him great expense–but the expense has been cheerfully met–the pain has all been endured, and will not need to be endured again, and it will cost none the more if you accept than if you decline; and moreover still, let it be considered, Jesus Christ has not acted unwisely; He did not pay too much for the soul's redemption–not a pang more than the interests of God's government demanded and the worth of the soul would justify.
–Charles Grandison Finney

CHARLES
GRANDISON
FINNEY
(1792-1875)

One day while simply reading the Bible alone in the woods, this young lawyer met Jesus Christ and abandoned his law practice for the evangelistic trail. Over 500,000 would respond to his homespun, dramatic appeals for salvation, many during the "nine mighty years" of 1824-1832, during which he conducted meetings all over the eastern United States and saw entire cities swept into revival. He later became a professor at and president of Oberlin College in Ohio, but continued revival preaching until his death at age eighty-three.

# FORGIVING A WRONG

THE SENSE OF JUSTICE IS MOST KEENLY FELT AMONG HUMAN BEINGS. INJUSTICE IS MOST QUICKLY PERCEIVED WHEN WE BELIEVE THAT SOMEONE HAS DONE WRONG TO US. A NEW CHRISTIAN WHO HAD CONVERTED FROM ANOTHER RELIGION EXPRESSED SURPRISE AT THE CONCEPT OF FORGIVENESS—BOTH FROM GOD TO HUMAN BEINGS AND AMONG HUMAN BEINGS. HE OBSERVED THAT IT WAS SOMETHING FROM BEYOND THIS WORLD.

## Luke 6:27-35

"But I tell you who hear me: Love your enemies, do good to those who hate you, bless those who curse you, pray for those who mistreat you. If someone strikes you on one cheek, turn to him the other also. If someone takes your cloak, do not stop him from taking your tunic. Give to everyone who asks you, and if anyone takes what belongs to you, do not demand it back. Do to others as you would have them do to you.

"If you love those who love you, what credit is that to you? Even 'sinners' love those who love them. And if you do good to those who are good to you, what credit is that to you? Even 'sinners' do that. And if you lend to those from whom you expect repayment, what credit is that to you? Even 'sinners' lend to 'sinners,' expecting to be repaid in full. But love your enemies, do good to them, and lend to them without expecting to get anything back. Then your reward will be great, and you will be sons of the Most High, because he is kind to the ungrateful and wicked. Be merciful, just as your Father is merciful."

PERSONALLY SPEAKING *As you consider the wrong that has been done to you, place it alongside the wrongs for which God has already granted you forgiveness. It looks different there.*

_____

_____

_____

_____

_____

_____

Consider the character of the person who has wronged you. He is either a good or a wicked man. If he is a good man, there is light and tenderness in his conscience, which sooner or later will bring him to a sense of the evil of what he has done. If he is a good man, Christ has forgiven him greater injuries than he has done to you; and why should not you forgive him? Will Christ not upbraid him for any of his wrongs, but frankly forgive them all; and will you take him by the throat from some petty abuse which he has offered you?

But if a wicked man has injured or insulted you, truly you have more reason to exercise pity than revenge toward him. He is in a deluded and miserable state; a slave to sin and an enemy to righteousness. If he should ever repent, he will be ready to make you reparation; if he continues impenitent, there is a day coming when he will be punished to the extent of his desserts. You need not study revenge. God will execute vengeance upon him.

–John Flavel

JOHN FLAVEL
(D. 1691)

John Flavel was an English Puritan educated at University College, Oxford. He served initially as a minister in an Anglican parish in Devon and later was lecturer at St. Saviour's in Dartmouth. His Nonconformist views brought about his dismissal from St. Saviour's. Flavel was then licensed as a Congregationalist. He was instrumental in promoting the union of Congregationalists and Presbyterians. He is best known today for his practical writings which are available in six volumes. One of his best known works is *Keeping the Heart*.

# WORSHIP SERVICE

RIDING UP TO CHURCH A FEW MINUTES LATE, YOU CAN SEE THEM THROUGH THE WINDOW. BUT WORSHIP CAN LOOK STRANGE WITH NO SOUND, WITHOUT THE FEELING OF BEING ON THE INSIDE. STEP INTO THE ROOM, HOWEVER, GET YOUR STUFF SET DOWN, AND PRETTY SOON IT FEELS RIGHT. PRETTY SOON, IT STARTS TO FLOW. BECAUSE WHEN YOU'RE ON THE INSIDE, YOU UNDERSTAND. THIS IS WHAT SERVING GOD IS ALL ABOUT.

## Luke 7:36-38, 44-47a

*Now one of the Pharisees invited Jesus to have dinner with him, so he went to the Pharisee's house and reclined at the table.*

*When a woman who had lived a sinful life in that town learned that Jesus was eating at the Pharisee's house, she brought an alabaster jar of perfume, and as she stood behind him at his feet weeping, she began to wet his feet with her tears. Then she wiped them with her hair, kissed them and poured perfume on them....*

*Then he turned toward the woman and said to Simon, "Do you see this woman? I came into your house. You did not give me any water for my feet, but she wet my feet with her tears and wiped them with her hair. You did not give me a kiss, but this woman, from the time I entered, has not stopped kissing my feet. You did not put oil on my head, but she has poured perfume on my feet.*

*"Therefore, I tell you, her many sins have been forgiven–for she loved much."*

PERSONALLY SPEAKING *Close your eyes. Imagine your first day in heaven. The white robe. The majestic throne. The sense of total peace and freedom. Oh, worship Him right now the way you'll be doing it then.*

If the Lord is to be Lord, worship must have a priority in our lives. The first commandment of Jesus is, "Love the Lord your God with all your heart, and with all your soul, and with all your mind, and with all your strength" (Mark 12:30). The divine priority is worship first, service second. Our lives are to be punctuated with praise, thanksgiving, and adoration. Service flows out of worship. Service as a substitute for worship is idolatry. Activity is the enemy of adoration.

The primary function of the Levitical priests was to "come near to minister to me" (Ezek. 44:15). For the Old Testament priesthood, ministry to God was to precede all other work. And that is no less true of the universal priesthood of the New Testament. One grave temptation we all face is to run around answering calls to service without ministering to the Lord himself.

Today God is calling his Church back to worship. This can be seen in high church circles where there is a renewed interest in intimacy with God. It can be seen in low church circles where there is a new interest in liturgy. It can be seen everywhere in between these two. It is as if God is saying, "I want the hearts of my people back!" And if we long to go where God is going and do what God is doing, we will move into deeper, more authentic worship.

–Richard J. Foster

RICHARD J. FOSTER (1940-   )

He is a psychologist and lifelong Quaker whose emphasis on returning to the classic practices of the Christian faith—such as solitude, simplicity, prayer, and fasting—caught a receptive ear among the church with his best-selling *Celebration of Discipline*, calling on many of the teachings espoused by the classic authors in this book. He established the Renovaré program for spiritual renewal in 1988, which seeks to help Christian leaders restore the beauty and strength of the authentic disciplines to modern faith.

# WORTH ALL THE WORK

MAYBE SOME OF US STRUGGLE WITH LAZINESS BECAUSE OUR WORK NO LONGER SATISFIES.
INSTEAD OF FEELING A SENSE OF ACCOMPLISHMENT, WE MERELY FEEL USED UP AT THE END OF
THE DAY. MAYBE THAT'S WHY WE ESCAPE TO THE TV, THE SOFA, THE MAGAZINES. IF WE COULD
ONLY SEE WORK AS SOMETHING TO THROW OURSELVES INTO, INSTEAD OF EIGHT TO TEN HOURS
WE HAVE TO FIND A WAY TO LIVE AROUND. . . .

## 2 Thessalonians 3:6-12

In the name of the Lord Jesus Christ, we command you, brothers,
to keep away from every brother who is idle and does not live according to the teaching you received from us.

For you yourselves know how you ought to follow our example.
We were not idle when we were with you, nor did we eat anyone's
food without paying for it. On the contrary, we worked night and day,
laboring and toiling so that we would not be a burden to any of you.

We did this, not because we do not have the right to such help,
but in order to make ourselves a model for you to follow. For even
when we were with you, we gave you this rule: "If a man will not
work, he shall not eat."

We hear that some among you are idle. They are not busy; they
are busybodies. Such people we command and urge in the Lord Jesus
Christ to settle down and earn the bread they eat.

PERSONALLY SPEAKING *Nothing wrong with resting. But rest that merely serves
as an escape from what you should be doing doesn't really refresh. Ask God for
the momentum to get your work done first.*

---

---

---

---

---

The slothful man loses both this world and the next; for he bears no fruit and he profits not another. It is impossible for a man to gain virtue without diligence and great toil. When you can abide in a safe place, do not stand in a perilous place: he abides in a safe place who strives and suffers and works and toils through God, and for the Lord God, not through fear or punishment, or for a price, but for love of God. . . .

A worldly proverb says, "Never set an empty pot on the fire hoping your neighbor will come and fill it." And so likewise God wills that no grace be left empty; for the good God never gives a grace to any man that it be kept empty; rather he gives it that a man may use it to a profit of holy words. . . .

Believe me, my brothers, I can swear, of a truth, that the more a man flees and shuns the burden and the yoke of Christ, the more grievous he makes it to himself and the more heavily it weighs upon him, and the greater is the burden; but the more ardently a man takes up his burden, ever heaping up more weight of his own will, the lighter and the more pleasant he feels it to bear. Would to God that men would labor to win the good things of the body, since they would win also those of the soul.
–Francis of Assisi

FRANCIS OF ASSISI (1182-1226)

Francis was in his twenties before taking seriously the call of God. But when impressed to help rebuild a church in his Italian homeland, he sold his horse and about all he had to give to the cause. Such total generosity marked his entire life, as he took up begging to embark on a course of caring for the poor, as well as preaching brotherly love and repentance. He abdicated leadership of the Franciscan Order as it began shifting away from his original vision and spent the remainder of his days in solitude and prayer.

# TRUE FRIENDS

USED TO THINK THE WORDS PEER PRESSURE WOULD HAVE NO PLACE IN ADULTHOOD. NOT SO. THE WORDS OF WARNING WE GIVE TO OUR TEENAGERS ABOUT THE VALUE OF GOOD FRIENDSHIPS STILL APPLY TO US. WE STILL NEED FRIENDS WHO CALL US HIGHER, PEOPLE WE CAN SERVE ALONGSIDE WITH A COMMON GROUND OF CHRISTIAN PURPOSE. WE'LL PROBABLY RISE NO HIGHER THAN THE VALUES OF OUR CLOSEST FRIENDS.

## Psalm 133:1, 3b; 2 Timothy 3:1–5; Philippians 1:27

How good and pleasant it is when brothers live together in unity!… For there the LORD bestows his blessing, even life forevermore.…

But mark this: There will be terrible times in the last days. People will be lovers of themselves, lovers of money, boastful, proud, abusive, disobedient to their parents, ungrateful, unholy, without love, unforgiving, slanderous, without self-control, brutal, not lovers of the good, treacherous, rash, conceited, lovers of pleasure rather than lovers of God–having a form of godliness but denying its power.

Have nothing to do with them.…

Whatever happens, conduct yourselves in a manner worthy of the gospel of Christ. Then, whether I come and see you or only hear about you in my absence, I will know that you stand firm in one spirit, contending as one man for the faith of the gospel.

PERSONALLY SPEAKING *Thank God for the friends you have that make you more like Christ than more like the world. Or ask God to draw your heart to someone who can serve that purpose in your life.*

Love every one with the pure love of charity, but have no friendship save with those whose intercourse is good and true, and the purer the bond which unites you so much higher will your friendship be.

If your intercourse is based on science it is praiseworthy, still more if it arises from a participation in goodness, prudence, justice, and the like; but if the bond of your mutual liking be charity, devotion, and Christian perfection, God knows how very precious a friendship it is! Precious because it comes from God, because it tends to God, because God is the link that binds you, because it will last forever in Him. Truly it is a blessed thing to love on earth as we hope to love in Heaven, and to begin that friendship here which is to endure forever there.

I am not now speaking of simple charity, a love due to all mankind, but of that spiritual friendship which binds soul together, leading them to share devotions and spiritual interests, so as to have but one mind between them. Such as these may well cry out, "Behold, how good and joyful a thing it is, brethren, to dwell together in unity!" Even so, for the "precious ointment" of devotion trickles continually from one heart to the other, so that truly we may say that of such friendship the Lord promises His Blessing and life forevermore. To my mind all other friendship is but as a shadow with respect to this, its links mere fragile glass compared to the golden bond of true devotion.

–Francis de Sales

FRANCIS DE SALES
(1567-1622)

Francis began theological instruction in his homeland of France, but after embracing the ecclesiastical life, was appointed to a position in Geneva, Switzerland. There he devoted himself to preaching and became widely known for his diligence and zeal, as well as his kindness and holiness. "Love alone," he said, "will shake the walls of Geneva." He rose to bishop, but constrained himself to live in very humble surroundings, dispensing with the comforts of his office in order to provide more abundantly for the poor.

# More Than a Feeling

EVEN IN MARRIAGE, THE MOST INTIMATE EARTHLY RELATIONSHIP, THERE ARE POINTS ALONG THE WAY WHEN A HUSBAND OR WIFE MUST LOOK THEIR LIFELONG FRIEND IN THE FACE AND DECIDE TO LOVE THEM DESPITE THE WAY THEY FEEL AT THE MOMENT. OH, SOME IDEALISTIC OUTSIDER MIGHT THINK LOVE SHOULD BE ABLE TO BURN FOREVER ON ITS OWN FIRE AND EMOTION. BUT CHOOSING TO LOVE IS HOW LOVE REALLY SURVIVES.

## 2 Thessalonians 2:13b-17; Titus 2:11-14

God chose you to be saved through the sanctifying work of the Spirit and through belief in the truth. He called you to this through our gospel, that you might share in the glory of our Lord Jesus Christ.

So then, brothers, stand firm and hold to the teachings we passed on to you, whether by word of mouth or by letter. May our Lord Jesus Christ himself and God our Father, who loved us and by his grace gave us eternal encouragement and good hope, encourage your hearts and strengthen you in every good deed and word. . . .

For the grace of God that brings salvation has appeared to all men. It teaches us to say "No" to ungodliness and worldly passions, and to live self-controlled, upright and godly lives in this present age, while we wait for the blessed hope–the glorious appearing of our great God and Savior, Jesus Christ, who gave himself for us to redeem us from all wickedness and to purify for himself a people that are his very own, eager to do what is good.

PERSONALLY SPEAKING *If you've found yourself in a spiritual dry spell, make yourself keep putting one foot in front of the other. You have no idea where those faithful feet can take you, if God has anything to do with it.*

It is possible for our religion to lose its true center by becoming what we may call unduly subjective. Great stress may be laid on personal feeling, on the assurance of personal salvation. Questions may be freely asked, and answers expected, as to whether this or that religious emotion has been experienced, as to whether a person has found peace or gained assurance or is saved.

Now peace with God and joy in believing, even assurance of a present state of salvation, are endowments of the Christian life, which God habitually bestows–which may be both asked for and thankfully welcomed. But they are not meant either to be the tests of reality in religion, or generally subjects of self-examination.

What our Lord claims of us first is service–the service of ready wills, then developing faith, and lives gradually sanctified by correspondence with Him. On these points we must rigorously examine ourselves, but the sense of the service of Another, of cooperation with Another, is meant to become so absorbing a consciousness as to swallow up in us the consideration of personal feeling, and at least to overshadow even the anxiety for our own separate salvation. By losing our lives in Christ and His cause, we are meant to save them; to serve Christ, not to feel Christ, is the mark of His true servants. They become Christians in proportion as they cease to be interested in themselves, and become absorbed in their Lord.
–Charles Gore

CHARLES GORE
(1853-1932)

After investing the first years of his professional life in academics in the Oxford area, this congenial Anglo-Catholic rose through religious office to become the first bishop of Birmingham. Though he held tightly to the episcopal system, he forged unifying relationships with non-Anglicans, evangelicals—even the civil authorities. He fared not so well as bishop of Oxford, where his calls to modernize the high church movement fell on resistant ears. He resigned in 1919, settling in London, continuing to write.

# HERE'S THE PLAN

WHAT WOULD YOU HAVE DONE IF YOU WERE GOD? BEFORE HE SPOKE THE FIRST DUST SPECK INTO BEING, HE COULD SEE DOWN THE CORRIDORS OF TIME TO ONE DARK AFTERNOON, ONE CRAGGY HILL, ONE ROUGHLY HEWN CROSS ABSORBING THE COSTLY BLOOD OF HIS PRIDE AND JOY. WOULD YOU HAVE STARTED THE BALL ROLLING? WOULD YOU HAVE THOUGHT IT WORTHWHILE? WOULD YOU BELIEVE HOW MUCH HE LOVES YOU?

## 1 Peter 1:18-25

*For you know that it was not with perishable things such as silver or gold that you were redeemed from the empty way of life handed down to you from your forefathers, but with the precious blood of Christ, a lamb without blemish or defect.*

*He was chosen before the creation of the world, but was revealed in these last times for your sake. Through him you believe in God, who raised him from the dead and glorified him, and so your faith and hope are in God.*

*Now that you have purified yourselves by obeying the truth so that you have sincere love for your brothers, love one another deeply, from the heart. For you have been born again, not of perishable seed, but of imperishable, through the living and enduring word of God.*

*For, "All men are like grass, and all their glory is like the flowers of the field; the grass withers and the flowers fall, but the word of the Lord stands forever." And this is the word that was preached to you.*

PERSONALLY SPEAKING *God had you in mind when He conceived His plan—your doubts, your sins, your struggles. But He gave till even a God could hurt. Give this day back to Him. He's already paid for it.*

God's love did not begin at the cross. It began in eternity before the world was established, before the time clock of civilization began to move. The concept stretches our minds to their utmost limits.

Can you imagine what God was planning when the earth was "without form and void"? There was only a deep, silent darkness of outer space that formed a vast gulf before the brilliance of God's throne. God was designing the mountains and the seas, the flowers and the animals. He was planning the bodies of His children and all their complex parts.

How could creation be by chance?

Even before the first dawn, He knew all that would happen. In His mysterious love He allowed it. The Bible tells us about the "Lamb that was slain from the creation of the world" (Rev. 13:8). God foresaw what His Son was to suffer. It has been said there was a cross in the heart of God long before the cross was erected at Calvary. As we think about it we will be overwhelmed at the wonder and greatness of His love for us.

–Billy Graham

BILLY GRAHAM
(1918-  )

Billy Graham was a fifteen-year-old boy in Charlotte, North Carolina, attending a revival led by Mordecai Ham in his local school, when the conviction of God gripped his heart and lit the first flames of what has become the greatest evangelistic ministry of all time. After marrying Ruth Bell in 1943, he began his worldwide gospel tours, achieving such prominence in 1949 that he established the Billy Graham Evangelistic Association and began his trademark radio program, *The Hour of Decision*. The rest is history.

# COMING CLEAN

OF ALL THE GREAT THINGS ABOUT HEAVEN, ONE OF THE BEST WILL BE EXPERIENCING A FEELING WE'VE NEVER FULLY KNOWN—THE FREEDOM OF BEING TOTALLY UNTOUCHED BY TEMPTATION, FULLY DELIVERED FROM THE CHAINS OF SIN. THEN WE'LL BE ABLE TO LOOK INTO HIS FACE WITHOUT WORRYING ABOUT WHAT WE MIGHT STUMBLE OVER. WHY DID WE EVER THINK THAT ANYTHING COULD COMPARE WITH THIS?

## Judges 10:6a, 6c-8a, 10-16

*Again the Israelites did evil in the eyes of the LORD. . . . And because the Israelites forsook the LORD and no longer served him, he became angry with them. He sold them into the hands of the Philistines and the Ammonites, who that year shattered and crushed them. . . .*

*Then the Israelites cried out to the LORD, "We have sinned against you, forsaking our God and serving the Baals."*

*The LORD replied, "When the Egyptians, the Amorites, the Ammonites, the Philistines, the Sidonians, the Amalekites and the Maonites oppressed you and you cried to me for help, did I not save you from their hands? But you have forsaken me and served other gods, so I will no longer save you. Go and cry out to the gods you have chosen. Let them save you when you are in trouble!"*

*But the Israelites said to the LORD, "We have sinned. Do with us whatever you think best, but please rescue us now." Then they got rid of the foreign gods among them and served the LORD. And he could bear Israel's misery no longer.*

PERSONALLY SPEAKING *Unholy pleasures block the flow of God's blessing. What makes sin sound so much better than God's best? Why keep being fooled by a lie when pure joy lies within your reach?*

_____

_____

_____

_____

_____

_____

It is not to be expected that those can come to clearness about their interest [in Christ] whose heart condemns them for keeping up some known transgressions against the Lord, which they will not let go, neither are using the means which they know to be appointed by God for delivering them from it. Neither can those come to clearness who know some positive duty commanded them in their stations, which they deceitfully shift and shun, not closing cheerfully with it, or not willing to be led into it.

I do not deny but that men may on good grounds plead an interest in Christ in the case of prevailing iniquity: "Iniquities prevail against me" (Psa. 65: 3). But it is hard to be attained, if at all attainable, when the heart is dealing deceitfully, and entertaining known guile in any particular. Therefore, let people clear themselves of the particular, which they know too well. It is the thing which hinders them, marring their confidence and access in all their approaches unto God.

That which does ordinarily lead away the heart in time of religious duty, and the remembrance of which has power to enliven and quicken the spirits more than the remembrance of God, that which withstandeth men when they would lay hold on the promise, as God casteth up men's sins to them who are meddling with His covenant, that is the thing which does prevent the knowledge of a gracious state. Let it go, and it will be more easy to reach the knowledge of an interest in Christ.

–William Guthrie

WILLIAM GUTHRIE
(1620-1665)

He was among the Scottish religious wing known as the Protestors—an outspoken minority who resisted the heavy-handed demands of Charles II upon the churches of Scotland and framed the issue as a choice between obeying the state and obeying God. Still, Guthrie was able to survive the violent purge that followed, remaining at his pulpit another 12 years or so before being driven from his parish in 1664. He died a year later, remembered most notably now for his book, *The Christian's Great Interest.*

# ONE WORLD RELIGION

THIS IS THE STORY OF TWO POWERFUL KINGDOMS: ONE RULED BY JUSTICE, TRUTH, AND RIGHT-EOUSNESS—ONE RULED BY PLEASURE, PAIN, AND FEAR. YET MANY ARE THE CITIZENS OF THAT GREAT AND GLORIOUS KINGDOM WHO GROW TIRED OF ITS TREASURES AND LONG FOR THE BANKS OF THE OTHER WORLD, WHERE TANTALIZING WAVES CALL THEM IN DEEPER, WHERE PEOPLE FORGET WHAT KINGDOM THEY REALLY BELONG TO.

## 1 John 2:15-17; James 4:4-5; 1:27

*Do not love the world or anything in the world. If anyone loves the world, the love of the Father is not in him.*

*For everything in the world–the cravings of sinful man, the lust of his eyes and the boasting of what he has and does–comes not from the Father but from the world.*

*The world and its desires pass away, but the man who does the will of God lives forever. . . .*

*You adulterous people, don't you know that friendship with the world is hatred toward God? Anyone who chooses to be a friend of the world becomes an enemy of God. Or do you think Scripture says without reason that the spirit he caused to live in us envies intensely? . . .*

*Religion that God our Father accepts as pure and faultless is this: to look after orphans and widows in their distress and to keep oneself from being polluted by the world.*

PERSONALLY SPEAKING *Never let the way you stack up to others be your gauge of godliness. Slipping into the world's ways is too subtle for that. Stay in His Word, keep His face before you, and you'll never want to go back.*

_____

_____

_____

_____

_____

_____

We are often distressed by church members who ask, "Can I be a Christian and do this? Why cannot I do that? What is wrong with dancing, smoking, card playing?" etc. What they are really asking is, "How much like the world can I live and be a Christian? How near the precipice can I walk without going over? How far away from the Lord can I be and still get to Heaven?" Why do they not ask, "How far from the world can I live? How near the Lord? How much like Him?" Such people prefer the Borderline to Beulah Land.

Remember the Christian pilgrims at Vanity Fair: "And as they wondered at their apparel, so they did likewise at their speech; for few could understand what they said. They naturally spoke the language of Canaan; but they that kept the Fair were men of this world. So that from one end of the Fair to the other they seemed barbarians to each other."

How old-fashioned that sounds today when most church members major in how much like Vanity Fair they can both look and live! The Devil has scored a great triumph here: Vanity Fair has become a little churchy, singing hymns in its programs and speaking a good word for God; and the church has become very worldly, conforming to the age instead of condemning it by the contrast of godly conduct.

Are you a borderline case? It bespeaks love of the world, which does not coexist with love of the Father.
–Vance Havner

VANCE HAVNER
(1901-1986)

He was a home-spun preacher from Jugtown, North Carolina, who at age nine was already sending Christian essays to the county paper, and at twelve stood on a chair behind a pulpit in Hickory, North Carolina, to deliver his first sermon. With no degrees or diplomas, he took his first pastorate in 1924, but began traveling as a full-time evangelist in 1940—which he continued well into his nineties. He was known for his tight one-liners and humorisms that brought a simple freshness to Christian thinking.

# JUST KEEP IT STEADY

WE ARE ONE-WEEK WONDERS. THINGS THAT SEEM SO AWFUL TODAY, SO UNJUST, SO IMPOSSIBLE, CAN BRIGHTEN UP OVER THE WEEKEND AND MAKE US FORGET ALL THE FUSS WE MADE. WE CAN LEARN A GOOD LESSON FROM THOSE WHO DON'T LET THE HARD TIMES MAKE THEM TOO PANICKY OR THE SOFT TIMES TOO SELF-ASSURED. TRUST IN GOD IS AN EVERYDAY VALUE THAT WILL SEE US SAFELY ALL THE WAY.

### *Psalm 30:2-12*

*O LORD my God, I called to you for help and you healed me. O LORD, you brought me up from the grave; you spared me from going down into the pit.*

*Sing to the LORD, you saints of his; praise his holy name. For his anger lasts only a moment, but his favor lasts a lifetime; weeping may remain for a night, but rejoicing comes in the morning.*

*When I felt secure, I said, "I shall never be shaken." O LORD, when you favored me, you made my mountain stand firm; but when you hid your face, I was dismayed.*

*To you, O LORD, I called; to the Lord I cried for mercy: "What gain is there in my destruction, in my going down into the pit? Will the dust praise you? Will it proclaim your faithfulness? Hear, O LORD, and be merciful to me; O LORD, be my help."*

*You turned my wailing into dancing; you removed my sackcloth and clothed me with joy, that my heart may sing to you and not be silent. O LORD my God, I will give you thanks forever.*

PERSONALLY SPEAKING *No matter where you are on the roller coaster today– the jerky lifts that warn of impending freefall, or the thrilling spins that excite your senses–be sure of this: It'll all level out in the end.*

# CLASSIC *Insights*

Won't you read the twelve verses of this short thanksgiving Psalm? Some think David wrote it after he recovered from a serious illness that happened about the time of the dedication of his house. David said, "O Lord my God, I cried unto thee, and thou hast healed me." It was God who delivered him out of his troubles, who answered his prayers, and who turned his mourning into dancing. God's anger lasted only for a moment, and David's weeping only for a night. His sackcloth (his humble compliance to the divine providence) was loosed; his griefs were balanced; his fears were silenced; his comforts returned; and he was girded with gladness.

David's sudden sickness teaches us to rejoice as though we rejoiced not–we never know how near sickness may be to us. In the same way, David's sudden return to a happy condition teaches us to weep as though we wept not–we never know how soon the storm clouds may turn to sunshine for us.

When the clouds were turned to sunshine, David realized that it was God who gave him gladness in order that he might sing praises to Him. When God, in answer to our prayers, keeps us from being silent in the grave, we must not be silent in the land of the living; but we must be fervent and constant in praising God. With a heart full of love to God for His goodness to us, our humble prayer is: "O Lord my God, I will give thanks unto thee forever."
–Matthew Henry

MATTHEW HENRY
(1662-1714)

Sure of God's calling to preach but firm in his Nonconformist convictions, Matthew Henry was privately ordained in order to avoid the same fate as his father—forced from his pulpit in accordance with Britain's Act of Uniformity just days after young Henry's birth. Greatly influenced by the Puritans, he made exposition of the Scriptures the theme of his ministry, rising before dawn each day to write the commentary that bears his name. He completed through the book of Acts, with friends composing the rest from his copious notes.

# Unseen Servants

THE MOTHER OR FATHER WHO SLIPS BACK INTO HER CHILD'S BEDROOM LATE AT NIGHT, WHO REPOSITIONS THE COVERS HER BARE LEGS HAVE KICKED BACK, WHO CHECKS TO MAKE SURE HER WINDOW IS LOCKED, AND SLIDES TEDDY BACK UNDER HER ARM—THAT'S A PERSON WHO KNOWS THAT INVISIBLE CARE IS THE MOST PRECIOUS SERVICE OF ALL. BEING WILLING TO LOVE WHEN ONLY GOD KNOWS IT IS A TRUE VIRTUE.

## Matthew 6:1-4, 16-18

"Be careful not to do your 'acts of righteousness' before men, to be seen by them. If you do, you will have no reward from your Father in heaven.

"So when you give to the needy, do not announce it with trumpets, as the hypocrites do in the synagogues and on the streets, to be honored by men. I tell you the truth, they have received their reward in full. But when you give to the needy, do not let your left hand know what your right hand is doing, so that your giving may be in secret. Then your Father, who sees what is done in secret, will reward you. . . .

"When you fast, do not look somber as the hypocrites do, for they disfigure their faces to show men they are fasting. I tell you the truth, they have received their reward in full.

"But when you fast, put oil on your head and wash your face, so that it will not be obvious to men that you are fasting, but only to your Father, who is unseen; and your Father, who sees what is done in secret, will reward you.

PERSONALLY SPEAKING *Thomas á Kempis said, "Learn to be unknown." Learn to seek the out-of-the-way places, the tasks that won't get you called to the platform. Learn to love it when no one notices.*

_____

_____

_____

_____

_____

_____

Sometimes the Shepherd and Much-Afraid walked over patches of thousands of tiny little pink or mauve blossoms, each minutely small and yet all together forming a brilliant carpet, far richer than any seen in a king's palace.

"I have often wondered about the wild flowers," she said. "It does seem strange that such unnumbered multitudes should bloom in the wild places of the earth where perhaps nobody ever sees them and the goats and the cattle can walk over them and crush them to death. They have so much beauty and sweetness to give and no one on whom to lavish it, nor who will even appreciate it."

The look the Shepherd turned on her was very beautiful. . . . "I must tell you a great truth, Much-Afraid, which only the few understand. All the fairest beauties in the human soul, its greatest victories, and its most splendid achievements are always those which no one else knows anything about, or can only dimly guess at. . . . . Many a quiet, ordinary, and hidden life, unknown to the world, is a veritable garden in which Love's flowers and fruits have come to such perfection that it is a place of delight where the King of Love himself walks and rejoices with his friends. Some of my servants have indeed won great visible victories and are rightly loved and reverenced by other men, but always their greatest victories are like the wild flowers, those which no one knows about."
–Hannah Hurnard

HANNAH
HURNARD
(1905-1990)

The writer of the classic *Hinds' Feet on High Places* was born into a Quaker family in England with pacifist principles, was known as a quiet, timid girl, yet grew to become a multilingual medical missionary in Jerusalem—one of only twelve who remained in the Jewish area of besieged Jerusalem during the unsettling days of 1948 when Israel won its statehood. Her journals of those momentous months appear in the book *Watchmen on the Walls*. Her missionary career spanned fifty years.

# WHOLEHEARTED

WE SPEAK OF SALVATION AS THE DAY WE GAVE OUR LIFE TO CHRIST. BUT REALLY, THAT WAS THE DAY CHRIST GAVE HIS LIFE TO US, PLACING INSIDE US THE SEEDS OF ETERNAL LIFE. IT'S IN THE DAYS THAT FOLLOW, WHEN PARENTS GROW ILL, WHEN WORK BECOMES HARD, WHEN PEOPLE DISAPPOINT US, THAT WE LEARN TO REALLY PUT OUR LIVES IN HIS HANDS, TO UNDERSTAND THAT SACRIFICING OURSELVES IS LIFE'S GREATEST GAIN.

## 2 Chronicles 6:37-39; Ezekiel 11:19-20a; Jeremiah 24:7

"And if they have a change of heart in the land where they are held captive, and repent and plead with you in the land of their captivity and say, 'We have sinned, we have done wrong and acted wickedly'; and if they turn back to you with all their heart and soul in the land of their captivity where they were taken, and pray toward the land you gave their fathers, toward the city you have chosen and toward the temple I have built for your Name; then from heaven, your dwelling place, hear their prayer and their pleas, and uphold their cause. And forgive your people, who have sinned against you. . . ."

"I will give them an undivided heart and put a new spirit in them; I will remove from them their heart of stone and give them a heart of flesh. Then they will follow my decrees and be careful to keep my laws. . . ."

"I will give them a heart to know me, that I am the LORD. They will be my people, and I will be their God, for they will return to me with all their heart.

PERSONALLY SPEAKING *Who's been getting your best lately? Your family? Your job? Anyone? Try to pinpoint whatever's standing in the way of your going all-out as a servant of Christ. What's stopping you?*

_____

_____

_____

_____

_____

_____

There are stories of painters who have mixed their own blood with their paint. They probably are fanciful tales, but the idea is worth something at any rate. Until the very life stuff of the man goes into his task, until he grinds himself into his paint, his work will be ordinary and will lack the mark of inspiration.

What a splendid sight it is to see a young man, who has been drifting along with the flow of the current, and who has put no blood into his work, suddenly wake up and throw himself with passion into his daily task as though his life depended on doing it. Everybody discovers that something has happened. A new spirit has awakened. There is some power behind him. What is the explanation? He is in love. He has found an inspiration. He is working for the sake of somebody, and this passion of love gives him joy as he works to make a home and a livelihood. His whole self goes into his task, because his life has become consecrated by love. His face shines, his eye flashes, his step is quick. When he puts his hand to a task, it moves, for there is power working in him.

We need to get a love which will melt down our lives and send the spirit of our entire personality into our work. We shall stop playing at religion, and the glow and rapture of service will make our faces shine when once, out of love, we pour into the task of saving the world all we are and all we have.
–Rufus Jones

RUFUS JONES
(1863-1948)

Unlike many of the other mystical thinkers of his time and the more distant past, this worldwide lecturer, author, and humanitarian believed that too much contemplation and withdrawal worked against the growth of spiritual fruit in a believer's life. As founder and a twenty-year chairman of the American Friends Service Committee, he felt that profound communion with Christ should result in a social responsibility, drawing on Christ's creative fullness and zeal to advance the purposes of God's kingdom on earth.

# GRACE THAT'S GREATER

GOD SEES OUR SIN FOR WHAT IT REALLY IS: A DISTORTION OF TRUTH, A PICKPOCKET OF PEACE, A DISTRACTION FROM THE REWARDS OF GOD'S ETERNAL THINGS. NO WONDER, THEN, IT GIVES HIM GREAT PLEASURE TO THROW THE WEIGHT FROM OUR SHOULDERS, TO WASH AWAY THE MUCK AND THE MIRE, TO PUT OUR FEET ON A ROCK AND A NEW SONG IN OUR HEARTS. NO WONDER HE HEARS EVERY TIME WE COME TO OUR SENSES.

## Romans 5:17-21

For if, by the trespass of the one man, death reigned through that one man, how much more will those who receive God's abundant provision of grace and of the gift of righteousness reign in life through the one man, Jesus Christ.

Consequently, just as the result of one trespass was condemnation for all men, so also the result of one act of righteousness was justification that brings life for all men.

For just as through the disobedience of the one man the many were made sinners, so also through the obedience of the one man the many will be made righteous.

The law was added so that the trespass might increase. But where sin increased, grace increased all the more, so that, just as sin reigned in death, so also grace might reign through righteousness to bring eternal life through Jesus Christ our Lord.

PERSONALLY SPEAKING *If you're been pressed out of measure by the temptations of the enemy, take heart in this: God's grace is even stronger, His hold on you is even tighter, His power in you is even mightier.*

Let us go, then, into the school of Calvary, with eyes and ears alert and quickened, that we may see and hear. We shall get into the secret places of the Most High, and we shall behold the marvelous unveiling of Infinite Love. We shall hear that wondrous evangel that Pascal heard, and which melted his heart, and hallowed all his years: "I love thee more ardently than thou hast loved thy sin."

I cannot describe the tremendous impact which that sentence makes upon my life. I know how I have sinned. I know how I have clung to my sin. I know how I have yearned after it. I know what illicit pleasure I have found in it. I know how I have pursued it at any cost. And, now, in the school of Calvary, my Master takes up this, my so strenuous and overwhelming passion for sin, and contrasts it disparagingly with His passion for me: "I love thee more than thou has loved thy sin." If in some quiet moment that grand evangel swept through our souls in heavenly strains, we should fall in love with the Lover, and our love would imply our entrance into eternal life.

–J. H. Jowett

JOHN HENRY
JOWETT
(1864-1923)

He studied at such esteemed universities as Edinburgh and Oxford and became a pastor in a number of well-known churches. He succeeded R. W. Dale at Carr's Lane Chapel in Birmingham, pastored the Fifth Avenue Presbyterian Church in New York City, and assumed the pulpit vacated by G. Campbell Morgan at Westminster Chapel in London. Along the way, he served as chairman of the Congregational Union and president of the National Free Church Council, while writing a number of devotional books.

# THE NATURE OF JUSTICE

SO HOW COULD A GOOD GOD CONDEMN WHAT WE MIGHT CONSIDER A GOOD PERSON TO A
SLOW, CRUEL, TORTUROUS ETERNITY? ISN'T THE BETTER QUESTION, HOW COULD HE NOT?
SHOULD A WORKER WHO FAILS TO MEET THE MOST BASIC EXPECTATIONS OF HIS EMPLOYER
EXPECT A PROMOTION? SHOULD A STUDENT WHO REJECTS HIS TEACHER'S AUTHORITY EXPECT TO
PASS? WHAT'S SO HARD TO UNDERSTAND HERE?

## Ezekiel 18:23-26a, 27, 29

*"Do I take any pleasure in the death of the wicked? declares the
Sovereign LORD. Rather, am I not pleased when they turn from their
ways and live?*

*"But if a righteous man turns from his righteousness and com-
mits sin and does the same detestable things the wicked man does,
will he live? None of the righteous things he has done will be remembered. Because of the unfaithfulness he is guilty of and because of the
sins he has committed, he will die.*

*"Yet you say, 'The way of the Lord is not just.' Hear, O house of
Israel: Is my way unjust? Is it not your ways that are unjust? If a
righteous man turns from his righteousness and commits sin, he will
die for it.... But if a wicked man turns away from the wickedness he
has committed and does what is just and right, he will save his
life....*

*"Yet the house of Israel says, 'The way of the Lord is not just.' Are
my ways unjust, O house of Israel? Is it not your ways that are
unjust?"*

PERSONALLY SPEAKING *Someone you know is—either deliberately or without
thinking—passing up the most generous offer made to human beings. Will you
spend some time praying that he'll see this offer for what it is?*

_____

_____

_____

_____

_____

_____

And that no one may say what is said by those who are deemed philosophers, that our assertions that the wicked are punished in eternal fire are big words and bugbears, and that we wish men to live virtuously through fear, and not because such a life is good and pleasant, I will briefly reply to this–that if this be not so, God does not exist; or if He exists, He cares not for men, and neither virtue nor vice is anything, and, as we have said before, lawgivers unjustly punish those who transgress good commandments.

But since these are not unjust, and their Father teaches them by the word to do the same things as Himself, they who agree with them are not unjust. And if one should object that the laws of men are diverse, and say that with some, one is considered good, another evil, while with others what seemed bad to the former is esteemed good, and what seemed good is esteemed bad, let him listen to what we say to this.

We know that the wicked angels appointed laws conformable to their own wickedness, in which the men who are like them delight; and the right Reason, when He came, proved that not all opinions nor all doctrines are good. Wherefore, I will declare the same and similar things to such men as these.

–Justin Martyr

JUSTIN MARTYR
(100-165)

He was taught in the schools of philosophy at Alexandria and Ephesus, but it was a "chance" conversation with an aged man along the seashore that opened his eyes to the truth of Christianity. After conversion, he continued to wear the cloak of the professional philosopher, but excelled at showing the proponents of pagan theology that the truth they partially understood was fully realized in Jesus Christ. He was arrested in Rome for practicing an unauthorized religion, refused to renounce his faith, and was beheaded.

# ULTIMATE VICTORY

SPURGEON ONCE REMARKED, AFTER HEARING ABOUT A CERTAIN NUMBER OF PEOPLE WHO HAD
BEEN SAVED DURING A REVIVAL MEETING, THAT IT WAS FOOLISH TO DECLARE IN A MOMENT WHAT
WOULD TAKE A WHOLE LIFETIME TO FULLY DETERMINE. YES, CHRIST SAVES US IN A MOMENT, AS
WE GENUINELY REPENT. BUT IT'S IN THE PROCESS OF LIFE, THROUGH FAILURE AND FAITHFULNESS,
THAT VICTORY SHOWS ITS COLORS.

## Ephesians 6:10-13; 2 Corinthians 10:3-5

*Finally, be strong in the Lord and in his mighty power. Put on the
full armor of God so that you can take your stand against the devil's
schemes.*

*For our struggle is not against flesh and blood, but against the
rulers, against the authorities, against the powers of this dark world
and against the spiritual forces of evil in the heavenly realms.*

*Therefore put on the full armor of God, so that when the day of
evil comes, you may be able to stand your ground, and after you
have done everything, to stand. . . .*

*For though we live in the world, we do not wage war as the world
does. The weapons we fight with are not the weapons of the world.
On the contrary, they have divine power to demolish strongholds.*

*We demolish arguments and every pretension that sets itself up
against the knowledge of God, and we take captive every thought to
make it obedient to Christ.*

PERSONALLY SPEAKING *Don't get too mad at yourself over small defeats. God's
not as concerned by how many times you fail as by how many times you fall
back into His grace, get back on your feet, and try again.*

Paul says that we are more than conquerors through faith. But can one do more than conquer? Yes, one can, if one stands after having conquered, preserves the victory, and abides in the victory.

How often has it not been seen that the one who had lifted a weight could not support the weight after having lifted it; or that the one who pressed victoriously against the storm without weakening, exhausted could not endure the calm which came with the victory; or the one who was so hardy he could endure all the changes of weather, heat and cold, but could not stand the strong breeze at the moment of victory! And how often has not a victory been won in vain, if the victor then became proud, conceited, arrogant, self-satisfied, and thus lost just through having conquered!

Spiritually understood, there are always two victories: a first victory, and then the second by which the first victory is preserved. The worldly always talks about one victory, the godly always talks about two. In the first conflict, he fought against the world for the victory which was won; in the second conflict he fights with God about that victory. A man only stands, then, after having overcome everything, when he immediately, at the very moment of victory, ascribes the victory to God. Oh, in the eyes of the world, what folly: to need God's assistance most of all after one has conquered!

–Søren Kierkegaard

SØREN
KIERKEGAARD
(1813-1855)

Much of this Danish philosopher's writing is harsh and introspective, reacting to the sterile, lukewarm, official Christianity of his day with a deep awareness of the personal demands of New Testament faith. Though he is regarded as one of the forerunners of existentialism, his rebellion against custom and fake idealism is grounded in an individual relationship with Jesus Christ, unlike the disenchanted, atheistic version of leaving men to determine their own morality. He died young, unmarried, his pen still ablaze.

# LOVE YOUR ENEMIES

FOR MOST OF US, OUR ENEMIES DON'T COME AT US WITH COURT ORDERS AND BUTCHER KNIVES, BUT WITH SNIDE REMARKS, PETTY COMPLAINTS, SOUR DISPOSITIONS. PERHAPS, THOUGH, IT TAKES THE SAME BRAND OF COURAGE TO ANSWER BACK IN CONFIDENT LOVE TO AN OVERBEARING WINDBAG AS TO STAND ON PRINCIPLE AGAINST INJUSTICE AND PREJUDICED HOSTILITY. LOVING OUR ENEMIES GOES ALL THE WAY.

## 1 Peter 4:12-19

Dear friends, do not be surprised at the painful trial you are suffering, as though something strange were happening to you. But rejoice that you participate in the sufferings of Christ, so that you may be overjoyed when his glory is revealed. If you are insulted because of the name of Christ, you are blessed, for the Spirit of glory and of God rests on you.

If you suffer, it should not be as a murderer or thief or any other kind of criminal, or even as a meddler. However, if you suffer as a Christian, do not be ashamed, but praise God that you bear that name.

For it is time for judgment to begin with the family of God; and if it begins with us, what will the outcome be for those who do not obey the gospel of God? And, "If it is hard for the righteous to be saved, what will become of the ungodly and the sinner?"

So then, those who suffer according to God's will should commit themselves to their faithful Creator and continue to do good.

PERSONALLY SPEAKING *Are you under personal attack? God will give you the words to say or show you a more excellent way. But trust Him to use this situation to bring healing. And to make you stronger through love.*

To our most bitter opponents we say, "We shall match your capacity to inflict suffering by our capacity to endure suffering. We shall meet your physical force with soul force. Do to us what you will, and we shall continue to love you. . . . Bomb our homes and threaten our children, and we shall still love you. Send your hooded perpetrators of violence into our community at the midnight hour, and beat us and leave us half dead, and we shall still love you. But be you assured that we will wear you down by our capacity to suffer. One day we shall win freedom, but not only for ourselves. We shall so appeal to your heart and conscience that we shall win you in the process, and our victory will be a double victory."

Love is the most durable power in the world. This creative force, so beautifully exemplified in the life of our Christ, is the most potent instrument available in mankind's quest for peace and security. The great military leaders of the past have gone, and their empires have crumbled and burned to ashes. But the empire of Jesus, built solidly and majestically on the foundation of love, is still growing. . . . History is replete with the bleached bones of nations that refused to listen to him. May we hear and follow his words–before it's too late. May we solemnly realize that we shall never be true sons of our heavenly Father until we love our enemies and pray for those who persecute us.
–Martin Luther King, Jr.

**MARTIN LUTHER KING (1929-1968)**

Before becoming American history's most famous advocate for civil rights, he served as a pastor in Montgomery, Alabama, as well as co-pastor along with his father at Ebenezer Baptist Church in his hometown of Atlanta. He rose to prominence while leading movements to secure equal rights for African Americans by encouraging nonviolent, mass demonstrations. He received the Nobel Peace Prize in 1964, but remained both adored and hated. He was murdered at a Memphis, Tennessee, hotel in 1968.

# PAY ATTENTION

WHEN YOU THINK ABOUT THE GREATS OF CHRISTIAN FAITH DOWN THROUGH THE AGES—THE ONES YOU'D MOST LOVE TO BE LIKE—DO YOU THINK THEY'D HAVE EVER BEEN SATISFIED WITH A DAILY PRAYER LIFE LIMITED TO THE HISTORICAL EQUIVALENT OF OUR MORNING DRIVE TIME? OR THE LAST FEW MINUTES BEFORE SLEEP CLAIMED THEM FOR THE NIGHT? IF YOU WERE THE FATHER, IS THAT ALL YOU'D WANT FROM YOUR KIDS?

## Matthew 6:5-13

"And when you pray, do not be like the hypocrites, for they love to pray standing in the synagogues and on the street corners to be seen by men. I tell you the truth, they have received their reward in full.

"But when you pray, go into your room, close the door and pray to your Father, who is unseen. Then your Father, who sees what is done in secret, will reward you.

"And when you pray, do not keep on babbling like pagans, for they think they will be heard because of their many words. Do not be like them, for your Father knows what you need before you ask him.

"This, then, is how you should pray: 'Our Father in heaven, hallowed be your name, your kingdom come, your will be done on earth as it is in heaven. Give us today our daily bread. Forgive us our debts, as we also have forgiven our debtors. And lead us not into temptation, but deliver us from the evil one.'

PERSONALLY SPEAKING *If you're having a hard time keeping your head in your prayers, you're going to have to give yourself more time to quiet your thoughts . . . and to approach God with a ready, listening heart.*

_____

_____

_____

_____

_____

_____

That this be most reverently done, should provoke in us the consideration in whose presence we stand, to whom we speak, and what we desire; standing in the presence of the omnipotent Creator of heaven and earth, and of all the contents thereof; to whom assist and serve a thousand of angels, giving obedience to his eternal majesty; and speaking unto him who knoweth the secrets of our hearts, before whom dissimulation and lies are always odious and hateful, and asking that thing which may be most to his glory and to the comfort of our conscience.

But diligently should we attend, that such things as may offend his godly presence, to the uttermost of our power, may be removed. And first, that worldly cares and fleshly cogitations (such as draw us from contemplation of our God) be expelled from us, that we may freely without interruption call upon God.

Our adversary, Satan, at all times compassing us about, is never more busy than when we address and bend ourselves to prayer. O! How secretly and subtly creepeth he into our breasts, and calling us back from God, causeth us to forget what we have to do; so that frequently when we (with all reverence) should speak to God, we find our hearts talking with the vanities of the world, or with the foolish imaginations of our own conceit.

–John Knox

**JOHN KNOX**
**(1514-1572)**

John Knox was known as a warm, personable man, but his frequent brushes with both the religious and civic establishment in cities throughout Europe paint him in a much bolder light. A Scottish reformer of deep Christian conviction who counted Calvin among his closest friends, he criticized the Second Book of Common Prayer to the very face of the royal court in England, was removed from his pulpit in Frankfurt for a similar dispute, and drew the fire of Queens Mary and Elizabeth for arguing against their rights to leadership.

# HOLY VOCATIONS

YOU MAKE YOUR WORK HOLY JUST BY BEING THERE. NOT BECAUSE THE JOB IS NECESSARILY CHRISTIAN—WHETHER IT'S TEACHING OR FARMING OR REPAIRING BRAKES AND MUFFLERS. THE HOLY SPIRIT THAT GOES WITH YOU EVERYWHERE YOU GO IS THE SAME ONE WHO CAN SHINE HIS LIGHT THROUGH YOUR WORDS, HIS CONVICTION THROUGH YOUR RESPONSES, AND HIS STRENGTH THROUGH YOUR EFFORT AND INTEGRITY.

## Ephesians 6:5-6; Colossians 3:23-25; 1 Thessalonians 4:11-12

*Slaves, obey your earthly masters with respect and fear, and with sincerity of heart, just as you would obey Christ. Obey them not only to win their favor when their eye is on you, but like slaves of Christ, doing the will of God from your heart. . . .*

*Whatever you do, work at it with all your heart, as working for the Lord, not for men, since you know that you will receive an inheritance from the Lord as a reward. It is the Lord Christ you are serving. Anyone who does wrong will be repaid for his wrong, and there is no favoritism. . . .*

*Make it your ambition to lead a quiet life, to mind your own business and to work with your hands, just as we told you, so that your daily life may win the respect of outsiders and so that you will not be dependent on anybody.*

PERSONALLY SPEAKING *Feeling like you're treading water in the work you do, lost without a calling in a sea of secularism? You be faithful right where you are. God's using you in ways you don't even know.*

As a good Christian should consider every place as holy, because God is there, so he should look upon every part of his life as a matter of holiness, because it is to be offered unto God. The profession of a clergyman is an holy profession, because it is a ministration in holy things, an attendance at the altar. But worldly business is to be made holy unto the Lord, by being done as a service to Him, and in conformity to His Divine will.

For as all men, and all things in the world, as truly belong unto God, as any places, things, or persons, that are devoted to Divine service, so all things are to be used, and all persons are to act in their several states and employments, for the glory of God.

Men of worldly business, therefore, must not look upon themselves as at liberty to live to themselves, to sacrifice to their own humors and tempers, because their employment is of a worldly nature. But they must consider, that, as the world and all worldly professions as truly belong to God as persons and things that are devoted to the altar, so it is much the duty of men in worldly business to live wholly unto God, as it is the duty of those who are devoted to Divine service.

–William Law

WILLIAM LAW
(1686-1761)

The author of *A Serious Call to a Devout and Holy Life* got his start in writing after forsaking the ministry on principle, refusing to take the oath of allegiance to George I in 1714 and thereby losing his fellowship at Cambridge. He became a personal tutor in the household of Edward Gibbon, father of the British historian, and was soon recognized for his apologetic writings. He held devoutly to the Christian faith as the epitome of ethical and moral teaching and spent his final years establishing schools and charities.

# IN HIS IMAGE

YOU CAN GO TO CHURCH LIKE CLOCKWORK, AND COME AWAY WITH GOOD LESSONS ON YOUR OWN INADEQUACIES, YOUR OWN SHORTCOMINGS, YOUR OWN SELFISH REASONS FOR NOT . . . OH . . . LET'S SAY, VISITING IN THE HOSPITALS. AND THOSE ARE ALL GOOD THINGS WE PROBABLY ALL NEED TO HEAR. BUT IN ALL THE ARM-TWISTING AND REMINDERS, DON'T MISS THIS: GOD THINKS YOU'RE REALLY SPECIAL. DID YOU KNOW THAT?

## John 17:6, 20-24

"I have revealed you to those whom you gave me out of the world. They were yours; you gave them to me and they have obeyed your word. . . .

"My prayer is not for them alone. I pray also for those who will believe in me through their message, that all of them may be one, Father, just as you are in me and I am in you. May they also be in us so that the world may believe that you have sent me.

"I have given them the glory that you gave me, that they may be one as we are one: I in them and you in me. May they be brought to complete unity to let the world know that you sent me and have loved them even as you have loved me.

"Father, I want those you have given me to be with me where I am, and to see my glory, the glory you have given me because you loved me before the creation of the world."

PERSONALLY SPEAKING *God thought of you way ahead of time, knew every hour you'd waste, saw every shortcut you'd take to skirt by on His grace, and He still went ahead with you as planned. That deserves a thanks.*

Are not all lifelong friendships born at the moment when at last you meet another human being who has some inkling (but faint and uncertain even in the best) of that something which you were born desiring, and which, beneath the flux of other desires and in all the momentary silences between the louder passions, night and day, year by year, from childhood to old age, you are looking for, watching for, listening for?

Be sure that the ins and outs of your individuality are no mystery to Him; and one day they will no longer be a mystery to you. The mold in which a key is made would be a strange thing, if you had never seen a key: and the key itself a strange thing if you had never seen a lock. Your soul has a curious shape because it is a hollow made to fit a particular swelling in the infinite contours of the divine substance, or a key to unlock one of the doors in the house with many mansions. For it is not humanity in the abstract that is to be saved, but you—you, the individual reader, John Stubbs or Janet Smith.

Blessed and fortunate creature, your eyes shall behold Him . . . . Your place in heaven will seem to be made for you and you alone, because you were made for it—made for it stitch by stitch as a glove is made for a hand.

–C. S. Lewis

C. S. LEWIS
(1898-1963)

The widely read Anglican layman and professor burst on the literary scene in 1941 with his satirical *Screwtape Letters*, followed by a series of radio broadcasts that formed the basis for *Mere Christianity*. He wrote books at the rate of one or more a year, in nearly every conceivable genre: novels, children's books, theology, poetry—many designed to cleverly remove the thoughtless, cultural blinders from an agnostic age in order that its people might see the rational, logical, utterly acceptable idea of Christian faith.

# PRESENT TENSE OBEDIENCE

THAT PERSON WE'RE EXPECTING TO BE IN TEN MORE YEARS IS QUITE A GUY OR GIRL. THAT MIN-
ISTRY WE'RE GOING TO DEVOTE OURSELVES TO ONCE WORK SLACKS UP A LITTLE BIT IS GOING TO
REALLY MAKE QUITE A DIFFERENCE. THAT BOOK WE'RE GOING TO READ ONCE THE FINAL FOUR IS
OVER OUGHT TO HAVE QUITE AN IMPACT ON OUR LIVES. THAT KIND OF PUTTING OFF TILL
TOMORROW CAN BECOME QUITE HABIT FORMING.

## Romans 13:8, 11-14;
## 1 Thessalonians 5:6-8

Let no debt remain outstanding, except the continuing debt to
love one another, for he who loves his fellowman has fulfilled the
law. . . .

And do this, understanding the present time. The hour has come
for you to wake up from your slumber, because our salvation is nearer now than when we first believed.

The night is nearly over; the day is almost here. So let us put aside
the deeds of darkness and put on the armor of light. Let us behave
decently, as in the daytime, not in orgies and drunkenness, not in
sexual immorality and debauchery, not in dissension and jealousy.

Rather, clothe yourselves with the Lord Jesus Christ, and do not
think about how to gratify the desires of the sinful nature. . . .

So then, let us not be like others, who are asleep, but let us be
alert and self-controlled. For those who sleep, sleep at night, and
those who get drunk, get drunk at night. But since we belong to the
day, let us be self-controlled, putting on faith and love as a breast-
plate, and the hope of salvation as a helmet.

PERSONALLY SPEAKING *There's something you know you'll never do unless you
decide to do it right now–amid all your busy schedule, amid all your cares and
commitments. It's now. Or it's never. Tell the truth.*

Let us bend all our energies to serve God in the way he wishes. This remark is made so that we may avoid the mistake of him who wastes his time in idle daydreaming. Such a one says, "If I were to become a hermit, I would become a saint"; or "If I were to enter a monastery, I would practice penance"; or "If I were to go away from here, leaving friends and companions, I would devote long hours to prayer." If, If, If–all these if's! In the meantime such a person goes from bad to worse.

These idle fancies are often temptations of the devil, because they are not in accord with God's will. Hence we should dismiss them summarily and rouse ourselves to serve God only in that way which he has marked out for us. Doing his holy will, we shall certainly become holy in those surroundings in which he has placed us.

Let us will always and ever only what God wills; for so doing, he will press us to his heart. To this end let us familiarize ourselves with certain texts of sacred Scripture that invite us to unite ourselves constantly with the divine will.

–Alphonsus Liguori

ALPHONSUS LIGUORI
(1696-1787)

A crucial oversight in a legal case forced him to abandon his law career, but not without bringing a simple oratory to the priesthood, in sharp contrast to the pompous rhetoric of his day. He began as a mission preacher in his native Naples, but rose to become a bishop in 1762, staunchly attacking along the way the severe asceticism making the rounds in eighteenth-century France. Clement XIV wouldn't accept his resignation, even as ill health weakened his effectiveness. He finally retired at nearly eighty years of age.

# A Holier Matrimony

SOMETHING WONDERFUL HAPPENS WHEN WE GET MARRIED. ALL OF A SUDDEN, INSTEAD OF HAVING THE FULL BURDEN OF LOOKING AFTER OURSELVES, WE HAVE A WHOLE OTHER PERSON WHO'S LOOKING AFTER US FOR US. AND AS WE RECEIVE THE COMFORTS OF THEIR HELP AND PROVISION, WE GET THE CHANCE TO CARE FOR THEM IN THE SAME LOVING WAY. WE GIVE, WE RECEIVE. WE SEE THE CHRISTIAN FAITH IN MINIATURE.

## Ephesians 5:22-30

*Wives, submit to your husbands as to the Lord. For the husband is the head of the wife as Christ is the head of the church, his body, of which he is the Savior. Now as the church submits to Christ, so also wives should submit to their husbands in everything.*

*Husbands, love your wives, just as Christ loved the church and gave himself up for her to make her holy, cleansing her by the washing with water through the word, and to present her to himself as a radiant church, without stain or wrinkle or any other blemish, but holy and blameless.*

*In this same way, husbands ought to love their wives as their own bodies. He who loves his wife loves himself. After all, no one ever hated his own body, but he feeds and cares for it, just as Christ does the church–for we are members of his body.*

PERSONALLY SPEAKING *Christ has sought us out as His church to be wedded to Him in a union more intimate and alive than the bond we share in marriage. Sense His love around you today. It will truly last forever.*

[One] incomparable benefit of faith is that it unites the soul with Christ as a bride is united with her bridegroom. By this mystery, as the Apostle teaches, Christ and the soul become one flesh. And if they are one flesh and there is between them a true marriage–indeed the most perfect of all marriages, since human marriages are but poor examples of this one true marriage–it follows that everything they have they hold in common, the good as well as the evil. Accordingly the believing soul can boast of and glory in whatever Christ has, as though it were its own, and whatever the soul has Christ claims as his own.

Let us compare these and we shall see inestimable benefits. Christ is full of grace, life, and salvation. The soul is full of sins, death, and damnation. Now let faith come between them and sins, death, and damnation will be Christ's, while grace, life, and salvation will be the soul's; for if Christ is a bridegroom, he must take upon himself the things which are his bride's and bestow upon her the things that are his. If he gives her his body and very self, how shall he not give her all that is his? And if he takes the body of the bride, how shall he not take all that is hers?

–Martin Luther

MARTIN LUTHER
(1483-1546)

Luther admitted to being motivated toward religious faith after being knocked to the ground by a lightning bolt. But his was a vow he would have to fulfill the hard way. Sometime in his thirties, while going through the motions as a friar in Wittenberg, Germany, he came to a new understanding of justification by grace alone, and embarked on a fiery crusade of church reform that resulted in his being declared an outlaw by the German emperor, but a hero to many for translating the Bible into the German language.

# THE PURPOSE OF PRAYER

THE IDEA IS AS HUMBLING AS IT IS SIMPLE: IF WE DIDN'T REALIZE HOW MUCH WE NEEDED HIM, WE'D NEVER GO TO HIM ON OUR OWN. EVEN WHEN WE FIRST CAME TO CHRIST, WE CAME BECAUSE HE DREW US, HE BECKONED US. AND SOMETIMES STILL, HE HAS TO USE THE RIPPLES OF UNCERTAINTY IN OUR LIVES, THE SHAKING OF ALL OUR STABILITIES, TO DRAW US BACK. TO GET US HOME. TO MAKE US REMEMBER.

## Psalm 27:4, 7-10, 13-14, 1 Chronicles 16:10-11

*One thing I ask of the LORD, this is what I seek: that I may dwell in the house of the LORD all the days of my life, to gaze upon the beauty of the LORD and to seek him in his temple. . . .*

*Hear my voice when I call, O LORD; be merciful to me and answer me. My heart says of you, "Seek his face!" Your face, LORD, I will seek. Do not hide your face from me, do not turn your servant away in anger; you have been my helper.*

*Do not reject me or forsake me, O God my Savior. Though my father and mother forsake me, the LORD will receive me. . . .*

*I am still confident of this: I will see the goodness of the LORD in the land of the living. Wait for the LORD; be strong and take heart and wait for the LORD. . . .*

*Glory in his holy name; let the hearts of those who seek the LORD rejoice. Look to the LORD and his strength; seek his face always.*

PERSONALLY SPEAKING *What problem is headlining your prayer time each day, never totally leaving the back of your mind? As hard as you're hunting for answers, be sure your questions lead you back to Him.*

"But if God is so good as you represent Him, and if He knows all what we need, and better far than we do ourselves, why should it be necessary to ask Him for anything?"

I answer, What if He knows prayer to be the thing we need first and most? What if the main object in God's idea of prayer be the supplying of our great, our endless need–the need of Himself? Hunger may drive the runaway child home, and he may or may not be fed at once, but he needs his mother more than his dinner. Communion with God is the one need of the soul beyond all other need: prayer is the beginning of that communion, and some need is the motive of that prayer. . . .

So begins a communion, a talking with God, a coming-to-one with Him, which is the sole end of prayer, yea, of existence itself in its inifinite phases. We must ask that we may receive: but that we should receive what we ask in respect of our lower needs, is not God's end in making us pray, for He could give us everything without that. To bring His child to his knee, God withholds that we may ask.

–George MacDonald

GEORGE MACDONALD (1824-1905)

His attempt at being a pulpit minister in his Scottish homeland failed, the church members unable to tolerate his bold style of preaching. He spent the remainder of his life writing novels, fairy tales, poetry, and Christian essays, even delivering popular lectures that brought him to the U.S. in 1872 and caught the attention of Emerson and Whittier. He was not resoundingly popular in his own day, but C.S. Lewis "regarded him as my master," connecting with MacDonald's call to obedience without proof or answers.

# Return Policy

GOOD RETAILERS KNOW THAT IF THEIR CUSTOMERS BELIEVE THEY CAN BRING ANY PURCHASE BACK TO THE STORE—FOR ANY REASON, AT ANY TIME—AND BE MET WITH KINDNESS, BE HEARD AND UNDERSTOOD, AND RECEIVE A SATISFACTORY ANSWER TO THEIR PROBLEM, THEY'LL KEEP COMING BACK. LITTLE DO THE BIG DEPARTMENT STORES KNOW WHO GAVE THEM THE IDEA. GOD'S BEEN IN THE RETURN BUSINESS A LONG TIME.

## Psalm 9:9-10; Isaiah 49:14-17; 44:21-22

*The LORD is a refuge for the oppressed, a stronghold in times of trouble. Those who know your name will trust in you, for you, LORD, have never forsaken those who seek you. . . .*

*But Zion said, "The LORD has forsaken me, the Lord has forgotten me."*

*"Can a mother forget the baby at her breast and have no compassion on the child she has borne? Though she may forget, I will not forget you! See, I have engraved you on the palms of my hands; your walls are ever before me. Your sons hasten back, and those who laid you waste depart from you. . . ."*

*"Remember these things, O Jacob, for you are my servant, O Israel. I have made you, you are my servant; O Israel, I will not forget you. I have swept away your offenses like a cloud, your sins like the morning mist. Return to me, for I have redeemed you."*

PERSONALLY SPEAKING *If there's anything God loves more than your faithful devotion and service, it's your willingness to come back when shame and guilt would keep you away. Come on back today.*

_____

_____

_____

_____

_____

_____

O Lord of hosts, when I am buoyed up in the waters of Your grace, I find that I can neither fathom nor measure them, for Your mercies are greater than all Your works. Who, dear Lord, ever came to You with a pious heart and was rejected? Who ever sought You and found You not? Who ever sought help from You and did not obtain it? Who ever prayed for Your grace and did not receive it? Who ever called upon You without being heard? Yes, dear Lord, how many did You accept in grace who otherwise by Your stern justice merited otherwise?

Adam departed from You and believed the counsel of the serpent; he transgressed Your commandments and became a child of death before You. But Your fatherly kindness did not reject him. In grace You sought him, called and reproved him, covered his nakedness with coats of skin, and graciously comforted him with the promised seed.

Your fatherly grace did not forsake me, a miserable sinner, but in love received me, converted me to another mind, led me with the right hand, and taught me by the Holy Spirit until of my own choice I declared war upon the world, the flesh, and the devil, and renounced all my ease, peace, glory, desire, and physical prosperity, and willingly submitted to the heavy cross of my Lord Jesus Christ that I might inherit the promised kingdom with all the soldiers of God and the disciples of Christ.
–Menno Simons

**MENNO SIMONS**
**(1496-1561)**

By his twenties, he was serving as a parish priest near his Dutch hometown. But he was two years into the priesthood before he dared to read the Bible. Troubled by its teachings (as well as the writings of Luther and other reformers), he renounced his ties to the Catholic Church and was soon a leading figure in the Anabaptist movement, traveling the Netherlands and the German North Sea coasts organizing churches, preaching personal holiness, and espousing the tenets of his namesake . . . the Mennonites.

# GLORY, GLORY, HALLELUJAH

WE CAN KEEP OUR NOSES PRESSED SO HARD TO THE WINDOWS OF THIS WORLD, WE CAN PUT SO MUCH STOCK IN OUR OWN ABILITY TO WORSHIP AND SERVE, WE CAN BECOME SO FORGETFUL OF THE ETERNAL PURPOSES DISGUISED AS THIS ORDINARY DAY, THAT WE LOSE OUR SENSE OF GLORY. WE FORGET HOW REAL GOD ACTUALLY IS. WE LOSE SIGHT OF THE FACT THAT OUR PRAYERS ARE BEING HEARD IN HEAVENLY PLACES.

## Psalm 98:1-9

Sing to the LORD a new song, for he has done marvelous things; his right hand and his holy arm have worked salvation for him.

The LORD has made his salvation known and revealed his righteousness to the nations. He has remembered his love and his faithfulness to the house of Israel; all the ends of the earth have seen the salvation of our God.

Shout for joy to the LORD, all the earth, burst into jubilant song with music; make music to the LORD with the harp, with the harp and the sound of singing, with trumpets and the blast of the ram's horn–shout for joy before the LORD, the King.

Let the sea resound, and everything in it, the world, and all who live in it. Let the rivers clap their hands, let the mountains sing together for joy; let them sing before the LORD, for he comes to judge the earth. He will judge the world in righteousness and the peoples with equity.

PERSONALLY SPEAKING *Especially if it's been a while, you need to lift your head from the things you can touch, taste, and see–and bridge the invisible gap to the glories of God. He's here right now. Worship Him.*

In the gentle movement of the trees in the forest, can you not hear the stepping of God's feet? And can you not detect the movement of God's Spirit at this moment upon your hearts? Does not this quiet hush, this eagerness, indicate the presence of the skirts of the Eternal as they fall upon us?

The whole earth is full of God–all time, all space–and it is because God is here, because there is as much of the Holy Ghost in this place as ever there was in the upper room on the day of Pentecost, because the forces of God are unexhausted, because the mighty river of God which is full of water is flowing through this place, that you and I are certain of blessing.

I believe that if some people had been in that very upper room itself when the Holy Ghost descended, blinded by prejudice and passion and worldliness, they would have heard only a noise, they would have perceived no flame. If they had been with John on Patmos, they might have heard the break of the waves upon the rocks, but they never would have heard the harping of the angels. On the other hand, if Peter and John were sitting where you are now, their faces would be lighted up with supernatural light, and they would say: "Did you not see? Did you not hear? God is here. The great God has come down from the heavens to bless these people. They have asked for it. They have claimed it. God has promised, and He has come."

–F. B. Meyer

F. B. MEYER
(1847-1929)

He was preaching long before he had a pulpit. In fact, a housemaid who overheard him as a boy sermonizing to his younger brothers and sisters dated her conversion to that afternoon. But beyond being a fine British pastor, he had a zeal for helping the common man, meeting discharged convicts at the prison doors in order to help them start a new life, leading movements to close saloons and brothels (almost five hundred fell to his efforts), and organizing groups to care for unwed mothers, the poor, and others.

# The Wisdom in Obedience

OBEDIENCE IS THE FOUNDATION OF CHRISTIAN SUCCESS. WE CAN TALK ALL WE WANT ABOUT WHAT WE THINK OR BELIEVE, OR HOW OUR CHURCH DOES THIS OR THAT, BUT WHATEVER DOESN'T RESULT IN OBEDIENCE—AND THEN MORE OBEDIENCE—AND MORE OBEDIENCE AFTER THAT—IS A WASTE OF TIME AT BEST. AND A HARMFUL DISPLAY OF PRIDE AT THE WORST. WHEN FAITH IS GENUINE, YOU CAN SEE THE RESULTS.

## 2 Peter 1:4-11

*Through these he has given us his very great and precious promises, so that through them you may participate in the divine nature and escape the corruption in the world caused by evil desires.*

*For this very reason, make every effort to add to your faith goodness; and to goodness, knowledge; and to knowledge, self-control; and to self-control, perseverance; and to perseverance, godliness; and to godliness, brotherly kindness; and to brotherly kindness, love.*

*For if you possess these qualities in increasing measure, they will keep you from being ineffective and unproductive in your knowledge of our Lord Jesus Christ.*

*But if anyone does not have them, he is nearsighted and blind, and has forgotten that he has been cleansed from his past sins.*

*Therefore, my brothers, be all the more eager to make your calling and election sure. For if you do these things, you will never fall, and you will receive a rich welcome into the eternal kingdom of our Lord and Savior Jesus Christ.*

PERSONALLY SPEAKING *We really don't know yet what God could do with our faithful obedience. But wouldn't it be great to find out? Wouldn't this be a good day to start building yours up good and strong again?*

# CLASSIC *Insights*

*(Prior to his expulsion from Eden, Adam speaks to the angel Michael:)*

Henceforth I learn, that to obey is best, and love with fear the only God,

To walk as in his presence, ever to observe His providence, and on him sole depend.

Merciful over all his works, with good still overcoming evil, and by small, accomplishing great things,

By things deemed weak subverting worldly strong, and worldly wise by simply meek;

That suffering for truth's sake is fortitude to highest victory, and to the faithful–death, the gate of life;

Taught this by his example whom I now acknowledge my redeemer, ever blest.

*(The angel Michael replies to Adam:)*

Thou hast attained the sum of wisdom; hope no higher . . .

Only add deeds to thy knowledge, add faith, add virtue, patience, temperance,

Add love, the soul of all the rest. Then wilt thou not be loath to leave this Paradise,

But shall possess a paradise within thee, happier far.

–John Milton

JOHN MILTON
(1608-1674)

Milton was born in London and studied until nearly thirty years of age before making his first attempts at poetry, knowing that his greatest work still lay before him. He postponed his poetry, though, after the outbreak of Civil War, writing pamphlets and serving as a loyal Cromwell supporter. He was certain to fare badly during Restoration, but was surprisingly included in the general amnesty. Totally blind and in the midst of quiet retirement, he wrote his masterpiece *Paradise Lost* in 1667, followed by its sequel.

# FOLLOW THROUGH

THE WALLS AND DOORWAYS OF TWENTY CENTURIES HAVE OVERHEARD MAN'S DEEPEST DISCUS-
SIONS ON THE SECURITY OF THE BELIEVER. SOME THINK YOU COULDN'T SLIP OUT OF GOD'S
GRASP IF YOU TRIED, OTHERS THINK YOU DANGLE BY YOUR FINGERNAILS YOUR WHOLE LIFE IN A
SNIVELING APPEAL FOR MERCY. WHEREVER THE TRUTH LIES, ONE THING'S FOR SURE: WE'RE ALL
BETTER OFF LIVING OUT OUR MOST HOLY FAITH.

## 1 Corinthians 3:10-17

*By the grace God has given me, I laid a foundation as an expert builder, and someone else is building on it. But each one should be careful how he builds. For no one can lay any foundation other than the one already laid, which is Jesus Christ.*

*If any man builds on this foundation using gold, silver, costly stones, wood, hay or straw, his work will be shown for what it is, because the Day will bring it to light. It will be revealed with fire, and the fire will test the quality of each man's work.*

*If what he has built survives, he will receive his reward. If it is burned up, he will suffer loss; he himself will be saved, but only as one escaping through the flames.*

*Don't you know that you yourselves are God's temple and that God's Spirit lives in you? If anyone destroys God's temple, God will destroy him; for God's temple is sacred, and you are that temple.*

PERSONALLY SPEAKING *As you pray today, recommit yourself to a set-apart, purified, holy life—one that seeks to please God as if it were all up to you, yet eternally thankful that salvation is by His grace from first to last.*

_____

_____

_____

_____

_____

_____

# CLASSIC *Insights*

We see clearly from this that we may be saved, yet all our works burned up. I may have a wretched, miserable voyage through life, with no victory, and no reward at the end; saved, yet so as by fire, or as Job puts it, "with the skin of my teeth." I believe that a great many men will barely get to heaven as Lot got out of Sodom, burned out, nothing left, works and everything else destroyed.

It is like this: when a man enters the army, he is a member of the army the moment he enlists; he is just as much a member as a man who has been in the army ten or twenty years. But enlisting is one thing and participating in a battle another. Young converts are like those enlisted.

It is folly for any man to attempt to fight in his own strength. The world, the flesh, and the devil are too much for any man. But if we are linked to Christ by faith, and He is formed in us the hope of glory, then we shall get the victory over every enemy. It is believers who are overcomers. "Thanks be unto God, which always causeth us to triumph in Christ." Through Him we shall be more than conquerors.

–D. L. Moody

**D. L. MOODY**
(1837-1899)

He was saved through the influence of his Sunday School teacher in Boston, then left for Chicago where he succeeded as a traveling salesman. But soon the call of God was too strong to resist, and he threw himself into full-time ministry. In 1873 he sailed for the British Isles, beginning a two-year evangelistic tour that reached millions and paved the way for his regular crusades in major United States cities. Historians estimate that he traveled more than a million miles in his lifetime. He died in midstream.

# THE MAIN EVENT

INEVITABLY IN LIFE, YOU'LL BE FACED WITH THE BIG QUESTION OF WHETHER THERE'S A GOD RUN-NING THIS WHOLE THING AT ALL. IT MAY SNEAK OUT OF A TV DOCUMENTARY, OR THROUGH AN AGONIZING SEASON OF LIFE-OR-DEATH, OR IN SOME TOTALLY UNEXPECTED, WHERE-DID-THAT-COME-FROM EXPERIENCE. WHEN IT DOES, MAKE SURE YOU HAVE YOUR ANSWER WELL REHEARSED. MAKE SURE YOUR FAITH IS READY FOR ANYTHING.

## Isaiah 43:1, 5-7, 10-11

But now, this is what the LORD says—he who created you, O Jacob, he who formed you, O Israel: "Fear not, for I have redeemed you; I have summoned you by name; you are mine. . . .

"Do not be afraid, for I am with you; I will bring your children from the east and gather you from the west. I will say to the north, 'Give them up!' and to the south, 'Do not hold them back.' Bring my sons from afar and my daughters from the ends of the earth—every-one who is called by my name, whom I created for my glory, whom I formed and made. . . .

"You are my witnesses," declares the LORD, "and my servant whom I have chosen, so that you may know and believe me and understand that I am he. Before me no god was formed, nor will there be one after me. I, even I, am the LORD, and apart from me there is no savior."

PERSONALLY SPEAKING *Think of the people you know who've been willing to believe this foolish mystery. People who'd never steer you wrong in a million years. This thing is true. This God is real. This we know.*

_____

_____

_____

_____

_____

_____

It has never been possible for me to persuade myself that . . . we have somehow made our appearance to sojourn briefly on our tiny earth, solely in order to mount the interminable soap opera, with the same characters and situations endlessly recurring, that we call history. It would be like building a great stadium for a display of tiddly-winks, or a vast opera house for a mouth-organ recital.

There must be another reason for our existence and that of the universe than just getting through the days of our life as best we may; some other destiny than merely using up such physical, intellectual, and spiritual creativity as has been vouchsafed us. This, anyway, has been the strongly held conviction of the greatest artists, saints, philosophers and, until quite recent times, scientists, through the Christian centuries, who have all assumed that the New Testament promise of eternal life is valid, and that the great drama of the Incarnation which embodies it, is indeed the master drama of our existence. To suppose that these distinguished believers were all credulous fools whose folly and credulity in holding such beliefs has now been finally exposed, would seem to me to be untenable; and anyway I'd rather be wrong with Dante and Shakespeare and Milton, with Augustine of Hippo and Francis of Assisi, with Dr. Johnson, Blake and Dostoevsky, than right with Voltaire, Rousseau, Darwin, the Huxleys, Herbert Spencer, H. G. Wells and Bernard Shaw.

–Malcolm Muggeridge

MALCOLM
MUGGERIDGE
(1903-1990)

He was an oft-quoted, agnostic, British author, journalist, and media personality who initially embraced socialism as the cure of society's ills, but abandoned his views after seeing its ugly side up close during the Ukrainian famine of 1932-33. His conversion to Christian faith occurred gradually over a number of years, until he was finally received into the Catholic church in 1982—"picking up the threads of a lost life, responding to a bell that had long been ringing, taking a place at a table that had long been vacant."

# THE FRUIT OF THE VINE

EVERYONE KNOWS THAT WHEN BRANCHES ARE BROKEN, THEY NO LONGER RECEIVE THE STRENGTH OF THE TREE. AND THAT WHEN PEOPLE PULL AWAY FROM THEIR CHRISTIAN ROOTS, THEIR WORK NO LONGER ENJOYS THE NOURISHMENT OF GOD'S BLESSING. BUT JUST AS SURELY—EVEN IF YOUR GROWTH IS SEEMING SLOW, ALMOST UNDETECTABLE—IF YOU'RE CLINGING TO CHRIST, YOU'RE GUARANTEED TO BEAR HIS FRUIT.

## John 15:1-8

*"I am the true vine, and my Father is the gardener. He cuts off every branch in me that bears no fruit, while every branch that does bear fruit he prunes so that it will be even more fruitful. You are already clean because of the word I have spoken to you.*

*"Remain in me, and I will remain in you. No branch can bear fruit by itself; it must remain in the vine. Neither can you bear fruit unless you remain in me. I am the vine; you are the branches. If a man remains in me and I in him, he will bear much fruit; apart from me you can do nothing.*

*"If anyone does not remain in me, he is like a branch that is thrown away and withers; such branches are picked up, thrown into the fire and burned.*

*"If you remain in me and my words remain in you, ask whatever you wish, and it will be given you. This is to my Father's glory, that you bear much fruit, showing yourselves to be my disciples."*

PERSONALLY SPEAKING *He's promised to give you everything you need as you remain in Him, as you seek His face, as you come to realize your total dependence upon His strength. Stop and rest there right now.*

_____

_____

_____

_____

_____

_____

When a new graft is placed in a vine and it abides there, there is a twofold process that takes place. The first is in the wood. The graft shoots its little roots and fibers down into the stem, and the stem grows up into the graft, and what has been called the structural union is effected. The graft abides and becomes one with the vine, and even though the vine were to die, would still be one wood with it.

Then there is the second process, in which the sap of the vine enters the new structure, and uses it as a passage through which sap can flow up to show itself in young shoots and leaves and fruit. Here is the vital union. Into the graft which abides in the stock, the stock enters with sap to abide in it.

Many believers pray and long very earnestly for the filling of the Spirit and the indwelling of Christ, and wonder that they do not make more progress. The reason is often this, the "I in you" cannot come because the "abide in me" is not maintained.

"There is one body and one spirit." Before the Spirit can fill, there must be a body prepared. The graft must have grown into the stem, and be abiding in it before the sap can flow through to bring forth fruit. It is as in lowly obedience we follow Christ, even in external things, denying ourselves, forsaking the world, and even in the body seeking to be conformable to Him, as we thus seek to abide in Him, that we shall be able to receive and enjoy the "I in you." The work enjoined on us: "Abide in me," will prepare us for the work undertaken by Him: "I in you."

–Andrew Murray

ANDREW
MURRAY
(1828-1917)

This widely read writer of such devout works as *Abide in Christ* and 250 other Christian publications was a native South African and a long-time leader in the Dutch Reformed Church. Greatly influenced by William Law, he led a profound and prayerful devotional life, writing much for the spiritual guidance of new converts and maintaining a number of successful pastorates in his lifetime. He actively supported education, evangelism, and missions involvement, and wielded an international influence for the gospel.

_____

_____

_____

_____

_____

_____

# SUPREME SACRIFICE

RAISED ON COURTROOM DRAMAS AND CAR CHASES, OUR MINDS CAN GROW STALE ON THE STORY OF CHRIST'S DEATH. THAT'S WHY EASTER ALWAYS CATCHES PREACHERS WITH THE CHALLENGE OF PUTTING A NEW SPIN ON THE OLD AND FAMILIAR, AS THOUGH ANYTHING ELSE IS NEEDED TO REMIND US THAT WE DROVE HIM TO HIS DEATH. IF IT WAS ENOUGH TO SAVE OUR SOULS, ISN'T IT ENOUGH TO HOLD OUR ATTENTION?

## Luke 23:35-43

*The people stood watching, and the rulers even sneered at him. They said, "He saved others; let him save himself if he is the Christ of God, the Chosen One." The soldiers also came up and mocked him. They offered him wine vinegar and said, "If you are the king of the Jews, save yourself."*

*There was a written notice above him, which read:* THIS IS THE KING OF THE JEWS. *One of the criminals who hung there hurled insults at him: "Aren't you the Christ? Save yourself and us!"*

*But the other criminal rebuked him. "Don't you fear God," he said, "since you are under the same sentence? We are punished justly, for we are getting what our deeds deserve. But this man has done nothing wrong."*

*Then he said, "Jesus, remember me when you come into your kingdom." Jesus answered him, "I tell you the truth, today you will be with me in paradise."*

PERSONALLY SPEAKING *Look at your hands—strong and unscarred. At your feet—smooth and unbloodied. At your side—soft and unpierced. At your heart—distracted and unremembering?*

_____

_____

_____

_____

_____

_____

Since humanity must be judged, the Son of God suffered in His spirit, soul, and body on the cross for the sins of the world.

Man sins through his body and there enjoys the temporary pleasure of sin. The hands must be nailed, for they love to sin. The mouth must suffer, for it loves to sin. The feet must be pierced, for they love to sin. The brow must be crowned with a thorny crown, for it too loves to sin. All that the human body needed to suffer was executed upon His body.

Human souls have fully enjoyed the pleasure of sins; accordingly, in His soul Jesus would endure the pain of sins. He would rather drink the cup given Him by God than the cup which numbed consciousness. Because every man had enjoyed the apparent glory of sin, so the Savior must endure the real shame of sin.

Man's human spirit has so separated itself from God, exalted itself, and followed the evil spirit that man's spirit must be totally broken in order that it may no longer resist God and remain allied with the enemy. Forsaken by God, Christ thus suffered sin's bitterest pain, enduring in darkness the punitive wrath of God on sin without the support of the love of God or the light of His countenance.

The cross bears the sinner's judgment, proclaims the sinner's worthlessness, crucifies the sinner, and releases the life of the Lord Jesus. Henceforth, anyone who accepts the cross shall be born anew by the Holy Spirit and receive the life of the Lord Jesus.
–Watchman Nee

WATCHMAN NEE
(1903-1972)

Nee To Shen taught, wrote, and ministered in his Chinese homeland amid poor health and extreme poverty. He had contracted tuberculosis in early adulthood, followed by a lifelong heart condition. But he pressed on, often lying in bed until moments before a speaking engagement. He spent his final twelve years in a Chinese labor farm, leaving this wearily written paper under his pillow. "Christ is the Son of God who died for the redemption of sinners. This is the greatest truth in the universe. I die because of my belief in Christ."

# ABOVE THE LAW

SOMEWHERE BEYOND THE REALM OF DUTY FOR DUTY'S SAKE, BEYOND THE RIGORS OF SPIRITUAL DISCIPLINES, BEYOND THE EARSHOT OF SIN'S LIES AND DECEIT, EXISTS A PEACE AND CONTENTMENT, AN EXPERIENCE OF ALMOST EFFORTLESS OBEDIENCE, AND THE JOY OF SERVING CHRIST FOR NO OTHER REWARD THAN THE BEAUTY OF HIS HOLINESS. NOT EVERYONE FINDS SUCH FREEDOM IN THIS LIFE. BUT YOU KNOW THE ONES WHO DO.

## Matthew 5:17-20; Galatians 5:13-14

Do not think that I have come to abolish the Law or the Prophets; I have not come to abolish them but to fulfill them.

I tell you the truth, until heaven and earth disappear, not the smallest letter, not the least stroke of a pen, will by any means disappear from the Law until everything is accomplished.

Anyone who breaks one of the least of these commandments and teaches others to do the same will be called least in the kingdom of heaven, but whoever practices and teaches these commands will be called great in the kingdom of heaven.

For I tell you that unless your righteousness surpasses that of the Pharisees and the teachers of the law, you will certainly not enter the kingdom of heaven. . . .

You, my brothers, were called to be free. But do not use your freedom to indulge the sinful nature; rather, serve one another in love. The entire law is summed up in a single command: "Love your neighbor as yourself."

PERSONALLY SPEAKING *You'll be free in Christ when sin loses its luster and serving the Lord is all that matters. You won't get there in a day. But once you've gotten a taste, you'll know there's nothing better.*

_____

_____

_____

_____

_____

_____

We have much evidence in the whole of life and many analogies for this truth: that freedom over the law does not mean freedom from the law, but represents a plus, in which the disciplines of the law are transcended.

We speak of the grace or gracefulness of a good athlete, a skater or tennis player, for instance. The freedom and gracefulness of his movements is possible only if he has fully mastered the basic disciplines of his form of physical art. The grace of an artist–say of a violinist–expresses itself in the freedom to interpret a composition imaginatively after the disciplines of the art have been fully mastered. The graciousness of a hostess does not mean freedom from the conventions of civility, but freedom over them in the imagination and selflessness with which the hostess meets her guests.

Even the army, which is not supposed to know anything about grace beyond the disciplines which it administers, does not remain unconscious of the mysteries of grace. If it gives the soldier a medal for heroism, it cites him for bravery "beyond the call of duty." It knows, in other words, of a realm of grace which the "ought" is powerless to attain.
–Reinhold Niebuhr

REINHOLD
NIEBUHR
(1893-1971)

He cut his teeth in ministry as a pastor in Detroit, but left in 1928 for a faculty position at a New York seminary. Never content to be quiet about his convictions, he constantly weighed in on the day's debates through lectures and writings, often taking controversial stands, but always causing his hearers to think about their actions and beliefs. Yet for all his influence, he is most remembered for three simple lines he composed for the church in his Massachusetts summer home. Today it's called . . . the Serenity Prayer.

# A Safe Distance

CHRISTIANS ARE COMMANDED TO BE THE SALT OF THE EARTH, TO BE AN AGENT OF PURITY, OF PRESERVATION, SOMETIMES OF DISCOMFORT. WE ARE CALLED TO BE A LIGHT, A HOPE, A WITNESS. BUT SALT THAT NEVER GETS STORED IN A SAFE PLACE EVENTUALLY LOSES ITS GOD-ORDAINED PROPERTIES. LIGHT THAT STRETCHES ITSELF TOO FAR RUNS OUT OF EXTENSION CORD. TO BE OUT THERE, WE ALSO NEED TIME AWAY FROM THERE.

## 2 Corinthians 6:14–7:1

Do not be yoked together with unbelievers. For what do right-eousness and wickedness have in common? Or what fellowship can light have with darkness? What harmony is there between Christ and Belial? What does a believer have in common with an unbeliever? What agreement is there between the temple of God and idols?

For we are the temple of the living God. As God has said: "I will live with them and walk among them, and I will be their God, and they will be my people."

"Therefore come out from them and be separate, says the Lord. Touch no unclean thing, and I will receive you. I will be a Father to you, and you will be my sons and daughters, says the Lord Almighty."

Since we have these promises, dear friends, let us purify ourselves from everything that contaminates body and spirit, perfecting holiness out of reverence for God.

PERSONALLY SPEAKING *Check the balance on your ledger of Christian activities. Spending too much time in ministry can run down the batteries on your effectiveness. Know your limits. Know when to say when.*

_____

_____

_____

_____

_____

_____

The relation of the authority of Jesus Christ to the authority of culture is such that every Christian must often feel himself claimed by the Lord to reject the world and its kingdoms with their pluralism and temporalism, their makeshift compromises of many interests, their hypnotic obsession by the love of life and the fear of death.

The movement of withdrawal and renunciation is a necessary element in every Christian life, even though it be followed by an equally necessary movement of responsible engagement in cultural tasks. Where this is lacking, Christian faith quickly degenerates into a utilitarian device for the attainment of personal prosperity or public peace; and some imagined idol called by his name takes the place of Jesus Christ the Lord.

What is necessary in the individual life is required also in the existence of the church. If Romans 13 is not balanced by 1 John, the church becomes an instrument of the state, unable to point men to their transpolitical destiny and their suprapolitical loyalty; unable also to engage in political tasks, save as one more group of power-hungry or security-seeking men.

–Richard Niebuhr

RICHARD
NIEBUHR
(1894-1962)

Richard Niebuhr brought to Yale a wealth of experience as a seminary professor, college president, pastor, and author, and labored there successfully in the field of Christian ethics for more than thirty years. More scholarly than his elder brother, Reinhold, he used his platform as an academician and author to grapple with the hard issues of the Christian's role in society. He is best known for his well-balanced book, *Christ and Culture*, which echoed his desire for a healthy tension between the church and the world.

# WHAT A FELLOWSHIP

SOMEWHERE WE GOT THE IDEA THAT TO GET SOMEONE INTERESTED IN CHRISTIANITY, WE HAD TO TRICK THEM INTO THINKING HOW COOL IT WAS. IF WE WERE TO TELL THEM THE TRUTH—IF WE WERE TO HIT THEM RIGHT UP FRONT WITH THE TITHING AND TUESDAY NIGHT PRAYER MEET-INGS—WE'D LOSE THEM BEFORE THEY HAD A CHANCE TO WARM UP TO IT. WHAT ARE WE AFRAID OF? IS JESUS TOO MUCH FOR THEM TO TAKE?

## 1 John 1:1-7

That which was from the beginning, which we have heard, which we have seen with our eyes, which we have looked at and our hands have touched–this we proclaim concerning the Word of life. The life appeared; we have seen it and testify to it, and we proclaim to you the eternal life, which was with the Father and has appeared to us.

We proclaim to you what we have seen and heard, so that you also may have fellowship with us. And our fellowship is with the Father and with his Son, Jesus Christ. We write this to make our joy complete.

This is the message we have heard from him and declare to you: God is light; in him there is no darkness at all.

If we claim to have fellowship with him yet walk in the darkness, we lie and do not live by the truth. But if we walk in the light, as he is in the light, we have fellowship with one another, and the blood of Jesus, his Son, purifies us from all sin.

PERSONALLY SPEAKING *You've got nothing to be ashamed of in Jesus Christ. Nothing to apologize for, nothing to hide behind. Take His name into your world today, and see who's wanting something more from life.*

John in his First Epistle tells us in general what communion with God is. He assures Christians that the fellowship of believers "is with the Father and with his Son Jesus Christ." And to impress this doctrine on the minds of his readers, he says, "truly our fellowship is with the Father and with his Son Jesus Christ."

Christians in those days were poor and despised. Christian leaders were treated as the filth of the world. So to invite people to become Christians, to join in their fellowship and to enjoy the precious things they enjoyed, seemed to be the height of foolishness.

"What good thing will we get if we join up with these Christians? Are they inviting us to share in their troubles? Do they want us to be persecuted, reviled, and scorned and to suffer all kinds of evils?"

It is with these objections in mind that John writes. Notwithstanding all the disadvantages their fellowship lay under from a worldly point of view, yet in truth it was, and they would soon find it to be, very honorable, glorious, and desirable. For "truly," says John, "our fellowship is with the Father and with his Son Jesus Christ."

–John Owen

JOHN OWEN
(1616-1683)

One of the greatest of the Puritan fathers, Owen was admired by his friends as "the Calvin of England" during and after the Civil War years. A Parliamentary sympathizer, he served as Cromwell's chaplain on expeditions to Ireland and Scotland in 1649-51, then spent the following years as the chief architect of the Cromwellian State Church, writing influential books, and establishing reforms in the university. Finally forced from his pulpit in 1660, he led a small congregation out of his own home until his death.

# Uncommon Knowledge

ISN'T IT JUST LIKE THE WORLD AND THEIR WEIRDO RELIGIONS TO TAKE SOMETHING SO TRUE AND
ESSENTIAL FROM THE CHRISTIAN FAITH AND TWIST IT JUST ENOUGH TO MAKE IT OFFENSIVE TO
THE BIBLICAL MIND? THAT'S WHAT'S HAPPENED TO THE DISCIPLINE OF MEDITATION—THE PRAC-
TICE OF CHEWING ON A WORD, A PHRASE, A VERSE, TILL THE SPIRIT UNFOLDS ITS COLOR AND
TEXTURE, TURNING RAW FACTS INTO SPIRITUAL FOOD.

## Jeremiah 31:31-34; Isaiah 11:9

"The time is coming," declares the LORD, "when I will make a new
covenant with the house of Israel and with the house of Judah.

"It will not be like the covenant I made with their forefathers
when I took them by the hand to lead them out of Egypt, because
they broke my covenant, though I was a husband to them," declares
the LORD.

"This is the covenant that I will make with the house of Israel
after that time," declares the LORD. "I will put my law in their minds
and write it on their hearts. I will be their God, and they will be my
people.

"No longer will a man teach his neighbor, or a man his brother,
saying, 'Know the LORD,' because they will all know me, from the
least of them to the greatest," declares the LORD. "For I will forgive
their wickedness and will remember their sins no more. . . ."

They will neither harm nor destroy on all my holy mountain, for
the earth will be full of the knowledge of the LORD as the waters cover
the sea.

PERSONALLY SPEAKING It'll take some getting quiet, and a little getting used to.
But you'll love what God does in your mind, your soul, your spirit, when you give
His Word enough time to sink in.

_____

_____

_____

_____

_____

_____

How can we turn our knowledge *about* God into knowledge *of* God? The rule for doing this is demanding, but simple. It is that we turn each truth that we learn *about* God into matter for meditation *before* God, leading to prayer and praise *to* God.

Meditation is a lost art today, and Christian people suffer grievously from their ignorance of the practice. Meditation is the activity of calling to mind, and thinking over, and dwelling on, and applying to oneself, the various things that one knows about the works and ways and purposes and promises of God. It is an activity of holy thought, consciously performed in the presence of God, under the eye of God, by the help of God, as a means of communion with God. Its purpose is to clear one's mental and spiritual vision of God, and to let His truth make its full and proper impact on one's mind and heart. It is a matter of talking to oneself about God and oneself; it is, indeed, often a matter of arguing with oneself, reasoning oneself out of moods of doubt and unbelief into a clear apprehension of God's power and grace. Its effect is ever to humble us, as we contemplate God's greatness and glory, and our own littleness and sinfulness, and to encourage and reassure us—'comfort' us, in the old, strong, Bible sense of the word—as we contemplate the unsearchable riches of divine mercy displayed in the Lord Jesus Christ.

–J. I. Packer

J. I. PACKER
(1926-    )

Reformed theologian and prolific author, Packer was first confronted with the power of the Gospel during an Oxford chapel service, committing his life to Christ and his career to theology. He served as a curate in the Birmingham diocese for two years, followed by a series of positions at British universities before embarking in 1979 for Regent College in Vancouver, British Columbia, where he still teaches. *Knowing God* is among the thirty books and nearly three hundred major pieces of writing on his resumé.

# SHAKEN, NOT STIRRED

WE COME FROM A LONG LINE OF SURVIVORS—BELEAGUERED BELIEVERS WHO HAVE STOOD
UNDER THE WEIGHT OF CRUEL THREATS AND ATTACKS, WHO HAVE GRITTED THEIR TEETH AND
CLAIMED THEIR CHRIST EVEN WHEN IT MEANT SURRENDERING THEIR SOUL TO THE FIRE OR THEIR
HEAD TO THE BASKET. YET WITH MILLIONS KILLED AND MANY MORE SURE TO COME, THE CHURCH
SURVIVES. THE SONG OF THE SAVED GOES ON.

## Revelation 7:9, 13-17

*After this I looked and there before me was a great multitude that
no one could count, from every nation, tribe, people and language,
standing before the throne and in front of the Lamb. They were wear-
ing white robes and were holding palm branches in their hands. . . .*

*Then one of the elders asked me, "These in white robes–who are
they, and where did they come from?" I answered, "Sir, you know."*

*And he said, "These are they who have come out of the great
tribulation; they have washed their robes and made them white in
the blood of the Lamb. Therefore, they are before the throne of God
and serve him day and night in his temple; and he who sits on the
throne will spread his tent over them.*

*"Never again will they hunger; never again will they thirst. The
sun will not beat upon them, nor any scorching heat. For the Lamb
at the center of the throne will be their shepherd; he will lead them
to springs of living water. And God will wipe away every tear from
their eyes."*

PERSONALLY SPEAKING *Would you add to your prayer list the unknown names
of countless believers who serve our Lord at the risk of life and family in nations
around the world–even today–even right now?*

_____

_____

_____

_____

_____

_____

In the first age of the world, men were swept into every kind of misdeed, and yet there were men of God such as Enoch, Lamech, and others who patiently waited for the Messiah promised from the beginning of the world.

The Egyptians were full of idolatry and magic, and even the people of God were carried away by their example. Nevertheless, Moses and others believed in God, who they had not seen, fixing their attention upon the eternal gifts he was preparing for them.

The Greeks, and afterwards the Romans, set up false gods. Their poets evolved a hundred different systems of theology, while their philosophers split up into a thousand different schools of thought. And yet in the heart of Judea, there were always chosen men who foretold the coming of that Messiah, which was revealed only to them. The Messiah himself came at length in the fullness of time, and since then we have seen so many schisms and heresies arise, so many nations overthrown, so many changes of every kind, while the church which worships him has always endured and continued without a break.

What is marvelous, unique, and altogether divine is that this religion which has always survived has also always been under attack. The fact that she has survived without ever yielding to the will of a tyrant suggests that her laws may have to yield to necessity, but [they] still transcend circumstances.

–Blaise Pascal

BLAISE PASCAL
(1623–1662)

His father, a widower moved the family to Paris when Pascal was eight and chose to educate his children at home, passing along a love for learning that would captivate Pascal his entire life. He devised the first calculator and discovered the physics principle that set the stage for modern hydraulics. But after his radical conversion in 1654, he devoted his energies to writing an apology on Christian faith. He died before he could finish, at only thirty-nine, but his notes are preserved for the ages in the classic *Pensées*.

# LIFE AND DEATH

TO BE ABLE TO LOOK BACK WITH FEW REGRETS, TO KNOW THAT YOU SPENT YOUR BEST DAYS GIVING CHRIST AND HIS CAUSE EVERYTHING YOU HAD, TO BE ABLE TO SAY WITH CONFIDENCE THAT YOU'D FOUGHT A GOOD FIGHT, YOU'D FINISHED THE COURSE, YOU'D KEPT THE FAITH . . . WHAT MORE PEACEFUL WAY TO APPROACH THE END THAN TO KNOW THAT THE ONE YOU'VE LOVED IS THE ONE WHO WAITS TO BE LOVED EVEN MORE?

## *2 Corinthians 4:8-11, 14, 16-18*

*We are hard pressed on every side, but not crushed; perplexed, but not in despair; persecuted, but not abandoned; struck down, but not destroyed.*

*We always carry around in our body the death of Jesus, so that the life of Jesus may also be revealed in our body. For we who are alive are always being given over to death for Jesus' sake, so that his life may be revealed in our mortal body . . . because we know that the one who raised the Lord Jesus from the dead will also raise us with Jesus and present us with you in his presence. . . .*

*Therefore we do not lose heart. Though outwardly we are wasting away, yet inwardly we are being renewed day by day. For our light and momentary troubles are achieving for us an eternal glory that far outweighs them all.*

*So we fix our eyes not on what is seen, but on what is unseen. For what is seen is temporary, but what is unseen is eternal.*

PERSONALLY SPEAKING *Try viewing each of your life's decisions in the light of eternity, determining whether a choice for God or a choice for self will be the one you'll have wanted to make when you look back later.*

I know perfectly well that poverty and misfortune becomes me better than riches and pleasures. For Christ the Lord, too, was poor for our sakes; and I, unhappy wretch that I am, have no wealth even if I wished for it. Daily I expect murder, fraud, or captivity, or whatever it may be; but I fear none of these things because of the promises of heaven. I have cast myself into the hands of God almighty. . . .

And if ever I have done any good for my God whom I love, I beg Him to grant me that I may shed my blood with those exiles and captives for His name, even though I should be denied a grave, or my body be woefully torn to pieces limb by limb by hounds or wild beasts, or the fowls of the air devour it. I am firmly convinced that if this should happen to me, I would have gained my soul together with my body, because on that day without doubt we shall rise in the brightness of the sun, that is, in the glory of Christ Jesus our Redeemer, as sons of the living God and joint heirs with Christ, to be made conformable to His image; for of Him, and by Him, and in Him we shall reign. . . .

I pray [that] whosoever deigns to look at or receive this writing which Patrick, a sinner, unlearned, has composed in Ireland should ever say that it was my ignorance if I did or showed forth anything however small according to God's good pleasure; but let this be your conclusion, and let it so be thought– as is the perfect truth–that it was the gift of God. This is my confession before I die.

–Patrick of Ireland

**PATRICK OF IRELAND**
**(390-461)**

He was born in Scotland, then captured at fourteen and taken to Ireland as a slave. There he called out to God and escaped at twenty years of age. But in a dream, he sensed God leading him to return to Ireland. So he entered the priesthood, was ordained as a bishop, and was commissioned to Ireland in 433. He boldly preached the gospel, converting thousands, including kings and their entire families, and died after years of poverty and hardship. He used the shamrock, his enduring symbol, to explain the Trinity.

# NEVER A DULL MOMENT

WE'VE BEEN READING THE BIBLE SO LONG, WE CAN SOMETIMES YAWN THROUGH THE STORIES OF WATER INTO WINE, DEMONS INTO PIGS, FISH INTO ATM MACHINES. BUT EVERY NOW AND THEN, EVEN WE SEASONED SAINTS WILL RUN ACROSS ONE OF JESUS' SAYINGS—LIKE AN INVISIBLE HAND REACHING THROUGH THE PAGES AND POINTING OUT A NEW PRINCIPLE. HIS WORD MAY BE FAMILIAR, BUT NEVER LOW ON SURPRISES.

## Matthew 13:10-12, 14-17

*The disciples came to him and asked, "Why do you speak to the people in parables?" He replied, "The knowledge of the secrets of the kingdom of heaven has been given to you, but not to them. Whoever has will be given more, and he will have an abundance. Whoever does not have, even what he has will be taken from him. . . ."*

*"In them is fulfilled the prophecy of Isaiah: 'You will be ever hearing but never understanding; you will be ever seeing but never perceiving. For this people's heart has become calloused; they hardly hear with their ears, and they have closed their eyes. Otherwise they might see with their eyes, hear with their ears, understand with their hearts and turn, and I would heal them.'*

*"But blessed are your eyes because they see, and your ears because they hear. For I tell you the truth, many prophets and righteous men longed to see what you see but did not see it, and to hear what you hear but did not hear it."*

PERSONALLY SPEAKING *As you come in close to the Word today, be on the lookout for something new and refreshing. You may have walked this way a hundred times before, but there's beauty in the details.*

_____

_____

_____

_____

_____

_____

So that is the outline of the official story–the tale of the time when God was the underdog and got beaten, when He submitted to the conditions He had laid down and became a man like the men He had made, and the men He had made broke Him and killed Him. This is the dogma we find so dull–this terrifying drama of which God is the victim and hero.

If this is dull, then what, in Heaven's name, is worthy to be called exciting? The people who hanged Christ never, to do them justice, accused Him of being a bore–on the contrary; they thought Him too dynamic to be safe. It has been left for later generations to muffle up that shattering personality and surround Him with an atmosphere of tedium.

We have very efficiently pared the claws of the Lion of Judah, certified Him "meek and mild," and recommended Him as a fitting household pet for pale curates and pious old ladies. To those who knew Him, however, He in no way suggested a milk-and-water person; they objected to Him as a dangerous firebrand. . . .

He was emphatically not a dull man in His human lifetime, and if He was God, there can be nothing dull about God either.

–Dorothy Sayers

DOROTHY
SAYERS
(1893-1957)

The daughter of an English clergyman, she graduated with honors at Oxford, but began her career as an advertising copywriter in London. Her passion, though, was mystery novels. She began her Wimsey series in 1923 and continued it most of her life, to much success. A difficult home life, however, drove her back to her spiritual roots, and she returned to more scholarly pursuits, writing religious dramas and Christian apologetics. She died before finishing a decade-long translation of Dante's *Divine Comedy*.

# AND LIBERTY FOR ALL

THE HUMAN MIND AND SPIRIT REBELS AGAINST HAVING ONLY ONE CHOICE. THERE SHOULD BE A MENU OF OPTIONS, A MULTI-TIERED PLAN THAT TAKES INTO ACCOUNT THE NUMEROUS VARIABLES INVOLVED. BUT WHEN ALL OF MAN'S EXCUSES ARE PEELED AWAY, THERE'S ONLY ONE SOURCE TO ALL HIS PROBLEMS (HIS ESCALATING DEBT OF SIN) AND ONLY ONE SUITABLE MEDICINE TO MATCH (A SINLESS SACRIFICE) . . . SORRY.

## Acts 4:8-12; Ephesians 2:17-18; 1 Timothy 2:5-6

*Then Peter, filled with the Holy Spirit, said to them: "Rulers and elders of the people! If we are being called to account today for an act of kindness shown to a cripple and are asked how he was healed, then know this, you and all the people of Israel: It is by the name of Jesus Christ of Nazareth, whom you crucified but whom God raised from the dead, that this man stands before you healed. He is 'the stone you builders rejected, which has become the capstone.'*

*"Salvation is found in no one else, for there is no other name under heaven given to men by which we must be saved. . . ."*

*He came and preached peace to you who were far away and peace to those who were near. For through him we both have access to the Father by one Spirit. . . .*

*For there is one God and one mediator between God and men, the man Christ Jesus, who gave himself as a ransom for all men—the testimony given in its proper time.*

PERSONALLY SPEAKING *God's perfect plan does seem foolish to those who insist on trying to reason it out. But to eyes opened by faith, His plan is astounding in its simplicity. Thank God today for making a way.*

The only way to become a Christian is neither by trying to live some sort of a Christian life nor by hoping for some sort of religious experience, but rather by accepting Christ as Savior. No matter how complicated, educated, or sophisticated we may be, or how simple we may be, we must all come the same way, insofar as becoming a Christian is concerned.

As the kings of the earth and the mighty of the earth are born in exactly the same way physically as the simplest man, so the most intellectual person must become a Christian in exactly the same way as the simplest person. This is true for all men, everywhere, through all space and all time. There are no exceptions. Jesus said a totally exclusive word: "No man cometh unto the Father but by me."

The reason for this is that all men are separated from God because of their true moral guilt. God exists, God has a character, God is a holy God, and when men sin they have a true moral guilt before the God who exists. That guilt is not just the modern concept of guilt feelings, a psychological guilty feeling in man. It is true moral guilt before the infinite, personal, holy God. Only the finished, substitutionary work of Christ upon the cross as the Lamb of God–in history, space, and time–is enough to remove this.

–Francis Schaeffer

FRANCIS
SCHAEFFER
(1912-1984)

He was prepared to enter adulthood as an agnostic, but forced himself to read the Bible before making up his mind. Six months later he was convinced, and embarked on a life of convincing thousands more. After moving his family to Switzerland in the late '40s, he formally opened his chalet in Huemoz as a home for Bible study and searching hearts. He called it L'Abri. Through his teaching and writing—24 books in all—he revealed how the Bible alone answers the most troubling problems of human life.

# For Love of Money

MONEY HAS A WAY OF SPINNING AN IMAGINARY NET UNDER THE TIGHTROPE OF OUR LIVES, A PORTFOLIO OF PENSIONS AND SECURITIES THAT GIVES US A FALSE SENSE OF LASTING SAFETY, AND HOLDS US DANGEROUSLY ALOOF FROM THE PROVISION OF GOD. HE KNOWS THAT WHEN THERE'S MONEY IN THE BANK, WE'RE LIKELY TO SPEND LESS TIME ON OUR KNEES AND HAVE LESS OF AN INCENTIVE TO SEE THE NET FOR WHAT IT REALLY IS.

## Luke 16:10-15

"Whoever can be trusted with very little can also be trusted with much, and whoever is dishonest with very little will also be dishonest with much.

"So if you have not been trustworthy in handling worldly wealth, who will trust you with true riches? And if you have not been trustworthy with someone else's property, who will give you property of your own?

"No servant can serve two masters. Either he will hate the one and love the other, or he will be devoted to the one and despise the other. You cannot serve both God and Money."

The Pharisees, who loved money, heard all this and were sneering at Jesus. He said to them, "You are the ones who justify yourselves in the eyes of men, but God knows your hearts. What is highly valued among men is detestable in God's sight."

PERSONALLY SPEAKING *God has no desire to separate you from your money— unless your money is starting to separate you from Him. Learn to see money as a tool, not a treasure. Be rich in what really matters.*

_____

_____

_____

_____

_____

_____

What is the test of Christian discipleship? Is it not the same as in Christ's own time? Have our surroundings modified or changed the test? If Jesus were here today, would he not call some of the members of the church to do just what he commanded the young man, and ask them to give up their wealth and literally follow him? I believe he would do that if he felt certain that any church member thought more of their possessions than the Savior. The test would be the same today as then. I believe Jesus would demand–He does demand now–as close a following, as much suffering, as great self-denial as when he lived in person on the earth. . . .

What would be the result if in this city every church member should begin to do as Jesus would do? It is not easy to go into details of the result. But we all know that certain things would be impossible that are now practiced by church members. What would Jesus do in the matter of wealth? How would he spend it? What principle would regulate his use of money? Would he be likely to live in great luxury and spend ten times as much on personal adornment and entertainment as he spent to relieve the needs of suffering humanity? How would Jesus be governed in the making of money?
–Charles Sheldon

**CHARLES SHELDON**
(1857-1946)

He was born in Wellsville, New York, held pastorates in both Kansas and Vermont, and was editor-in-chief of the *Christian Herald* from 1920-1925. But even those unfamiliar with his name certainly know by now his 100-year-old book—the classic *In His Steps* that tells the semi-fictional account of a church compelled to judge their daily decisions by the question, "What would Jesus do?" Because it was never copyrighted, numerous publishers have reprinted his story over the years, reaching millions of readers.

# TIME SENSITIVE

FOR SOME REASON, WE HAVE TO BE UNDER THE GUN TO REALIZE HOW PRECIOUS TIME IS. WE HAVE TO BE TWO DAYS FROM LEAVING HOME FOR COLLEGE BEFORE WE DISCOVER HOW SWEET ARE THE SOUNDS OF PLATES CLATTERING IN THE KITCHEN OR DAD'S CAR PULLING UP IN THE DRIVEWAY. TIME IS RUNNING SHORT. THE PEOPLE WE LOVE ARE GROWING OLDER. THE PROMISES WE'VE MADE MUST BE ACTED ON.

### Psalm 103:15-16; 90:9-10; James 4:13-17

*As for man, his days are like grass, he flourishes like a flower of the field; the wind blows over it and it is gone, and its place remembers it no more. . . .*

*All our days pass away under your wrath; we finish our years with a moan. The length of our days is seventy years–or eighty, if we have the strength; yet their span is but trouble and sorrow, for they quickly pass, and we fly away. . . .*

*Now listen, you who say, "Today or tomorrow we will go to this or that city, spend a year there, carry on business and make money." Why, you do not even know what will happen tomorrow.*

*What is your life? You are a mist that appears for a little while and then vanishes. Instead, you ought to say, "If it is the Lord's will, we will live and do this or that."*

*As it is, you boast and brag. All such boasting is evil. Anyone, then, who knows the good he ought to do and doesn't do it, sins.*

PERSONALLY SPEAKING *It's time–time to get busy moving your life in the direction God wants you to go. Time to say the things you've been wanting to say. Time to understand you don't have that much time.*

The Master [says]: Many there are who have wasted the precious time given to them for My service, but even now there is an opportunity for them to rouse themselves and make the best use of the time that remains to them. They are like a hunter who, while wandering in the jungle, picked up some pretty stones on the bank of a stream. Unaware of their value he used them one by one in his sling to shoot at the birds seated on the trees near the river, and so one by one they fell into the water and were lost. With one still in his hand he returned to the city, and as he passed along the bazaar a jeweler caught sight of it, and told the silly fellow that it was a valuable diamond for which he could get thousands of rupees. When he heard this he began to bewail himself and say, "Woe is me! I didn't know their value, and have been using many of these diamonds to shoot at birds by the riverside, and they have fallen into the river and are lost, otherwise I should have been a millionaire. Still I have saved this one, and that is something gained."

Every day is like a precious diamond, and though many priceless days have been wasted in the pursuit of fleeting pleasures, and are for ever sunk in the depths of the past, you should awake to the value of what remains, and bringing it into the best possible use, gather for yourself spiritual riches. Use it in My service, who have given to you life and all its priceless blessings, and by using them to save others from sin and death you will obtain an everlasting and heavenly reward.

–Sadhu Sundar Singh

**SADHU SUNDAR SINGH**
(1889-1929)

He was a model Sikh: lover of the holy books, of meditation, of good works. And fanatically hostile to Christianity, once burning a Bible in public to express his outrage. His father, already concerned about his son's religious zeal, disapproved even of this act, and Sadhu made plans to kill himself. But even while making ritual preparation for his own death, he was overcome by Christ's reality in a vision and devoted the remainder of his life to preaching the gospel in a humble style, literally around the world.

# FACE TO FACE

HE'S RIGHT HERE. IN THIS ROOM. WHAT WE DON'T NOTICE FOR THE REFRIGERATOR HUMMING IS THAT GOD IS MORE REAL IN THIS PLACE THAN THE PICTURES ON THE WALL. THE WORDS WE SPEAK IN PRAYER ARE NOT ONLY TO SOUND PIOUS AND HOLY. THE SONGS WE SING IN WORSHIP ARE NOT SO WE CAN FOLLOW THE TENOR LINE IN THE HYMNBOOK. THEY'RE BEING HEARD BY A REAL GOD . . . WHO'S RIGHT HERE IN THIS ROOM.

## 1 John 3:1a, 2-3; Colossians 3:1-4; Job 19:25-27

How great is the love the Father has lavished on us, that we should be called children of God! And that is what we are! . . . Dear friends, now we are children of God, and what we will be has not yet been made known. But we know that when he appears, we shall be like him, for we shall see him as he is. Everyone who has this hope in him purifies himself, just as he is pure. . . .

Since, then, you have been raised with Christ, set your hearts on things above, where Christ is seated at the right hand of God. Set your minds on things above, not on earthly things. For you died, and your life is now hidden with Christ in God. When Christ, who is your life, appears, then you also will appear with him in glory. . . .

I know that my Redeemer lives, and that in the end he will stand upon the earth. And after my skin has been destroyed, yet in my flesh I will see God; I myself will see him with my own eyes—I, and not another. How my heart yearns within me!

PERSONALLY SPEAKING *Try this. Every hour on the hour, make yourself take about fifteen seconds to remember you're in the presence of God. Never let His face out of your sight, not even for a minute.*

_____

_____

_____

_____

_____

_____

Because God is not visibly present to the eye, it is difficult to feel that a transaction with Him is real. I suppose if when we made our acts of consecration we could actually see Him present with us, we should feel it to be a very real thing, and would realize that we had given our word to Him and could not dare to take it back, no matter how much we might wish to do so. Such a transaction would have to us the binding power that a spoken promise to an earthly friend always has to a man of honor.

We need to see that God's presence is a certain fact always, and that every act of our soul is done right before Him, and that a word spoken in prayer is as really spoken to Him as if our eyes could see Him and our hands could touch Him. Then we shall cease to have such vague conceptions of our relations with Him, and shall feel the binding force of every word we say in His presence.

Sight is not faith. Hearing is not faith. Neither is feeling faith. But believing when we can neither see, hear, nor feel, is faith. Therefore, we must believe before we feel, often against our feelings, if we would honor God by our faith. He who believes has assurance. He who doubts does not. But how can we doubt since His very command tells us to present ourselves a living sacrifice to Him? He has pledged to receive us.

–Hannah Whitall Smith

HANNAH WHITALL SMITH (1832-1911)

She was born into a pious family in Pennsylvania, but underwent years of skepticism before she was converted in 1858. Then in 1867, she experienced a refreshing in her spiritual walk that led her to a total commitment to Christ, a life of spiritual victory best explained in her well-known book, *The Christian's Secret to a Happy Life*. She and her husband traveled and spoke at Christian meetings, helping in 1874 to begin the Keswick Convention, an annual English meeting of Bible teaching that is still active today.

# A REAL RESURRECTION

WE ARE NEARER GOD'S RETURN THAN WE'VE EVER BEEN BEFORE. THE THINGS WE READ IN REVELATION MAY SEEM A MILLION MILES AWAY, BUT ONE DAY THEY'LL BE HERE AND NOW, AND THE PRIZE OF OUR REDEMPTION WILL BE RIGHT BEFORE OUR EYES. WOULDN'T IT CHANGE OUR WORSHIP IF WE WERE TRULY WATCHING? WOULDN'T IT UNLOCK THE WORDS WE'VE LEFT UNSAID IF WE HAD ONE EAR TO THE HEAVENS . . . WAITING?

## 1 Corinthians 15:12-14, 16-20, 58

But if it is preached that Christ has been raised from the dead, how can some of you say that there is no resurrection of the dead? If there is no resurrection of the dead, then not even Christ has been raised. And if Christ has not been raised, our preaching is useless and so is your faith. . . .

For if the dead are not raised, then Christ has not been raised either. And if Christ has not been raised, your faith is futile; you are still in your sins. Then those also who have fallen asleep in Christ are lost. If only for this life we have hope in Christ, we are to be pitied more than all men.

But Christ has indeed been raised from the dead, the firstfruits of those who have fallen asleep. . . .

Therefore, my dear brothers, stand firm. Let nothing move you. Always give yourselves fully to the work of the Lord, because you know that your labor in the Lord is not in vain.

PERSONALLY SPEAKING *The death of others grieves us, but unless we've smelled its foul breath ourselves, we can only imagine the fear. Yet underneath the human emotions, are you sure of resurrection? You can be.*

_____

_____

_____

_____

_____

_____

Christ's resurrection is a high and sovereign consolation against death. Death, we know, is the grand enemy of mankind, the merciless tyrant over nature, and the king of terrors. But, blessed be God, Christ has given a mortal blow to his power, and broken his scepter. And if we, by a thorough conquest of our sins, and rising from them, can be but able to say, "O sin, where is thy power?" we may very rationally and warrantably say thereupon, "O death, where is thy sting?" So that, when we come to resign back these frail bodies, these vessels of mortality, to the dust, from whence they were taken, we may yet say of our souls as Christ did of the damsel whom he raised up, that she was not dead, but only slept; for, in like manner, we shall as certainly rise out of the grave, and triumph over the dishonors of its rottenness and putrefaction, as we rise in the morning out of our beds, with bodies refreshed, and advanced into higher and nobler perfections. For the head being once risen, we may be sure the members cannot stay long behind. And Christ is already risen and gone before, to prepare mansions for all those who belong to him under that high relation, "that where he is, they (to their eternal comfort) may be also, rejoicing and singing praises and hallelujahs to him who sitteth upon the throne, and to the Lamb for ever and ever."
–Robert South

ROBERT SOUTH
(1634–1716)

This Anglican clergyman was born in Hackney and educated at Oxford, where he became a public speaker in 1660. He accepted a royal chaplaincy, but declined any further office. Still, his sermons were among the classics of English divinity, rich in eloquence and skill, full of wit and precision, mingling what he considered the three integral elements of a good message—simplicity, clarity, and fervor. In fact, he was known as a stickler for excellence, reacting against the oratorical excesses of the Puritans.

# Rightful Places

We live beneath our privilege. When God talks about riches in glory, when we hear about weapons made mighty through prayer, when we sing about the wonder-working power in the blood, we're declaring things more true than all of our common sense put together. The price Jesus paid is total and complete, and we can walk in His victory every day, unafraid.

## Ephesians 2:1-7

As for you, you were dead in your transgressions and sins, in which you used to live when you followed the ways of this world and of the ruler of the kingdom of the air, the spirit who is now at work in those who are disobedient.

All of us also lived among them at one time, gratifying the cravings of our sinful nature and following its desires and thoughts. Like the rest, we were by nature objects of wrath.

But because of his great love for us, God, who is rich in mercy, made us alive with Christ even when we were dead in transgressions—it is by grace you have been saved.

And God raised us up with Christ and seated us with him in the heavenly realms in Christ Jesus, in order that in the coming ages he might show the incomparable riches of his grace, expressed in his kindness to us in Christ Jesus.

PERSONALLY SPEAKING *You have unclaimed prizes waiting for you, custom-made blessings that could be yours for the asking. What's keeping you too busy, what's charming you too much, to enjoy your inheritance?*

I am persuaded there are Christians as much in grace beyond ordinary Christians as ordinary Christians are beyond the profane. There are heights which common eyes have never seen, much less scaled. Oh! there are nests among the stars where God's own saints dwell, and yet how many of us are content to go creeping along like worms in the dust! Would that we had grace to cleave the clouds and mount into the pure blue sky of fellowship with Christ! We do not serve God as we should. We are cold as ice, when we should be like molten metal, burning our way through all opposition. We are like the barren Sahara, when we should be blooming like the garden of the Lord. We give to God pence, when he deserveth pounds; nay, deserveth our heart's blood to be coined in the service of his church and of his truth. Oh! we are but poor lovers of our sweet Lord Jesus; not fit to be his servants, much less to be his brides. If he had put us in the kitchen to be scullions, I fear we are scarce fit for the service; and yet he hath exalted us to be bone of his bone and flesh of his flesh, married to him by a glorious marriage covenant. O brethren! God often calleth us to higher degrees of piety, and yet we will not come.

–Charles Haddon Spurgeon

CHARLES
HADDON
SPURGEON
(1834-1892)

He was already a pastor at seventeen, and was called at age twenty to the New Park Street Baptist Chapel in London, where crowds soon necessitated the building of the Metropolitan Tabernacle in 1859. Over the years, nearly fifteen thousand were added into its membership, and he enlarged his vision to include a seminary (now Spurgeon's College), an orphanage, and other charitable agencies. His clear, impassioned preaching continues to inspire in repeated printings, as well as his *Treasury of David* and *Morning and Evening*.

# ALL EYES ON YOU

WE DON'T KNOW WHAT OTHER PEOPLE'S LIVES ARE REALLY LIKE. THE FACES WE SEE AT CHURCH OR AT WORK, EVEN THE PEOPLE WE KNOW ONLY THROUGH TV OR LOCAL POLITICS, MAY HIDE YEARS OF HARDSHIPS AND STRUGGLES THAT YOU'D NEVER KNOW FROM LOOKING AT THEM. GOD CERTAINLY TAKES A PERSON'S PAST INTO ACCOUNT. HE IS CERTAINLY PATIENT AND FULL OF MERCY. WHO DO WE THINK WE ARE NOT TO BE?

## Romans 14:10-13; Galatians 6:1-5

You, then, why do you judge your brother? Or why do you look down on your brother? For we will all stand before God's judgment seat. It is written: "'As surely as I live,' says the Lord, 'every knee will bow before me; every tongue will confess to God.'" So then, each of us will give an account of himself to God.

Therefore let us stop passing judgment on one another. Instead, make up your mind not to put any stumbling block or obstacle in your brother's way. . . .

Brothers, if someone is caught in a sin, you who are spiritual should restore him gently. But watch yourself, or you also may be tempted. Carry each other's burdens, and in this way you will fulfill the law of Christ.

If anyone thinks he is something when he is nothing, he deceives himself. Each one should test his own actions. Then he can take pride in himself, without comparing himself to somebody else, for each one should carry his own load.

PERSONALLY SPEAKING *Next time you feel a twinge of condescension, next time you get mad at what someone said or did, look the other way until you can look into their eyes with acceptance and forgiveness.*

_____

_____

_____

_____

_____

_____

A spiritual man must never be taking note of others, and above all of their sins; lest he fall into wrath, bitterness, and a judging spirit towards his neighbors. O children, this works such great mischief in a man's soul, it is miserable to think of it. As you love God, shun this evil temper, and turn your eyes full upon yourself to see if you can discover the same fault, either in times past or at present. And if you find it, remember how it is God's appointing that you should now behold this sin in another so you may be brought to acknowledge and repent of it.

Thus a good heart draws correction from the sins of others, and is guarded from all harsh judgment and wrath, and preserves an even temper, while an evil heart puts the worst interpretation on all that it sees and turns it to its own hurt. Thus a good man is able to maintain inviolate a due love and loyalty towards his fellow man.

This would often tend more to his neighbor's improvement than all the efforts he could make for it in the way of reproofs or chastisements, even if they were done in love (though we often imagine that our reproofs are given in love when it is in truth far otherwise). For I tell you, dear child, if you could conquer yourself by long-suffering and gentleness and the pureness of your heart, you would have vanquished all your enemies.

–Johannes Tauler

JOHANNES
TAULER
(1300-1361)

His was a simple method of preaching, delivered during a scary season of European history marked by earthquakes, civil war, financial crises. During the Black Death of 1347, which killed up to a half of countries' total populations, he devoted his ministry to the sick. Shortly thereafter, he and others in the Dominican order were driven from Germany to Switzerland at the pope's decree. But his message was always this: Look for what God is doing, sense the mystery of His grace, even in the midst of suffering.

# Something Beautiful

HE HAD DRIVEN THAT WAY BETWEEN WORK AND THE HOUSE, OH . . . MAYBE ONE THOUSAND TIMES. BUT THE DAY THE CAR RAN OUT OF GAS TWO MILES FROM HOME, HE WAS FORCED TO SEE HIS WELL-WORN PATH THROUGH NEW EYES. ON FOOT. HE PASSED FLOWER GARDENS AND LAWN SPRINKLERS, WATCHED A DOG CHASING A RABBIT, EVEN FOUND FIFTY-SEVEN CENTS FOR HIS LITTLE GIRL. IT'S AMAZING WHAT YOU MISS WHEN YOU FLY BY SO FAST.

## Psalm 1:1-2; 119:105-106, 109-112, 137-138, 140

*Blessed is the man who does not walk in the counsel of the wicked or stand in the way of sinners or sit in the seat of mockers. But his delight is in the law of the LORD, and on his law he meditates day and night. . . .*

*Your word is a lamp to my feet and a light for my path. I have taken an oath and confirmed it, that I will follow your righteous laws. . . .*

*Though I constantly take my life in my hands, I will not forget your law. The wicked have set a snare for me, but I have not strayed from your precepts.*

*Your statutes are my heritage forever; they are the joy of my heart. My heart is set on keeping your decrees to the very end. . . .*

*Righteous are you, O LORD, and your laws are right. The statutes you have laid down are righteous; they are fully trustworthy. . . . Your promises have been thoroughly tested, and your servant loves them.*

PERSONALLY SPEAKING *Spend enough time in the Scripture today for its depth and beauty to rise out of the ordinary and meet you like a friend you haven't seen in ten years. There's more in there than you realize.*

_____

_____

_____

_____

_____

_____

By regeneration the believer, having become the child of God, finds new interest and instruction in all the works of God. His Father designed and created them, upholds and uses them, and for His glory they exist. But this is peculiarly true of the Word of God.

Possessing the mind of Christ, instructed by the Spirit of Christ, he finds in every part of God's Word testimony to the person and work of his adorable Master and Friend. The Bible in a thousand ways endears itself to him, while unfolding the mind and ways of God. His past dealings with His people, and His wonderful revelations of the future.

While thus studying God's Word, the believer becomes conscious of a new source of delight; not only is that which is revealed precious, but the beauty and perfection of the revelation itself grows upon him. He has now no need of external evidence to prove its inspiration; it everywhere bears the impress of Divinity. And as the microscope which reveals the coarseness and blemishes of the works of man only shows more fully the perfectness of God's works, and brings to light new and unimagined beauties, so it is with the Word of God when closely scanned.

–Hudson Taylor

HUDSON TAYLOR
(1832–1905)

Hudson Taylor was born in England, but upon his conversion, his heart became strangely drawn to the closed empire of China. And he acted on it immediately, landing at Shanghai in 1854, only to find himself detached from his source of financial support. Living on prayer, adopting Chinese dress, and being happy for others to reap where he had sowed, he labored tirelessly in pursuit of the lost, establishing his own organization (China Inland Mission) which became known as the "shock troops" of evangelistic advance.

# WHAT A CHARACTER

THESE CLASSIC AUTHORS AND PREACHERS MAY NOT HAVE ALWAYS TALKED IN THE SAME HOLY TONES THEY WROTE WITH. SOME OF THEM PROBABLY WEREN'T ABOVE KICKING THE CAT OR MUTTERING AN OATH WHEN THEY PICKED UP A SPLINTER. BUT THE LEGACY OF VIRTUE THEY LEAVE BEHIND CASTS A STIRRING SHADOW OVER THE COMPLACENCY OF OUR DAY. HOW'D YOU LIKE TO HAVE A CHARACTER PEOPLE STILL TALK ABOUT?

## Titus 3:3-8

*At one time we too were foolish, disobedient, deceived and enslaved by all kinds of passions and pleasures. We lived in malice and envy, being hated and hating one another.*

*But when the kindness and love of God our Savior appeared, he saved us, not because of righteous things we had done, but because of his mercy.*

*He saved us through the washing of rebirth and renewal by the Holy Spirit, whom he poured out on us generously through Jesus Christ our Savior, so that, having been justified by his grace, we might become heirs having the hope of eternal life.*

*This is a trustworthy saying. And I want you to stress these things, so that those who have trusted in God may be careful to devote themselves to doing what is good. These things are excellent and profitable for everyone.*

PERSONALLY SPEAKING *When you get the time, see if it would be helpful for you to make a list of your own priorities, your own goals for your own character. Becoming the person you want to be is no accident.*

The humble man trusts not to his own discretion, but relies rather upon the judgment of his friends, counselors, or spiritual guides. He does not murmur against commands. He is not inquisitive into the reasonableness of indifferent and innocent commands, but believes their command to be reason enough in such cases to exact his obedience.

He lives according to a rule, and with compliance to public customs, without any affection or singularity. He is meek and indifferent in all accidents and chances. He patiently bears injuries. He is always unsatisfied in his own conduct, resolutions, and counsels. He is a great lover of good men, and a praiser of wise men, and a censurer of no man. He is modest in his speech, and reserved in his laughter.

He fears, when he hears himself commended, lest God make another judgment concerning his actions than men do. He gives no pert or saucy answers, when he is reproved, whether justly or unjustly. He loves to sit down in private, and, if he may, he refuses the temptations of offices and new honors. He is ingenuous, free, and open, in his actions and discourses. He mends his fault, and gives thanks, when he is admonished. He is ready to do good offices to the murderers of his fame, to his slanderers, backbiters, and detractors, as Christ washed the feet of Judas. And is contented to be suspected of indiscretion, so before God he may really be innocent.
–Jeremy Taylor

JEREMY TAYLOR
(1613-1667)

He was one of the last from the golden age of English preaching, called by one source "the Shakespeare of divines." His was a highly colorful, elaborate style, woven throughout with classical allusions and picturesque imagery. But it wasn't a grace formed by soft living. He had taken a controversial stance of allegiance to the king during the Civil War, which found him in prison three times under Puritan rule. But his loyalties were rewarded at the Restoration, and his rich writings lasted long after his death.

# HALLMARKS OF HUMILITY

ONE OF THE STRANGE THINGS ABOUT BECOMING A PERSON OF STRONG CHARACTER IS THAT YOU DON'T QUITE REALIZE IT WHEN YOU DO. AS LOVE, SELFLESSNESS, AND HUMILITY TAKE UP MORE PERMANENT RESIDENCE IN YOUR LIFE, WORSHIP, AND RELATIONSHIPS, OTHERS SEE WHAT YOU DON'T—BECAUSE POURING YOURSELF OUT MEANS EXCHANGING THE RUSH OF BEING NOTICED FOR THE BLUSH OF BEING A BLESSING.

## Philippians 2:5-9; 2 Corinthians 8:9; Matthew 20:26b-27

*Your attitude should be the same as that of Christ Jesus: Who, being in very nature God, did not consider equality with God something to be grasped, but made himself nothing, taking the very nature of a servant, being made in human likeness.*

*And being found in appearance as a man, he humbled himself and became obedient to death–even death on a cross!*

*Therefore God exalted him to the highest place and gave him the name that is above every name. . .*

*For you know the grace of our Lord Jesus Christ, that though he was rich, yet for your sakes he became poor, so that you through his poverty might become rich. . . .*

*Whoever wants to become great among you must be your servant, and whoever wants to be first must be your slave–just as the Son of Man did not come to be served, but to serve, and to give his life as a ransom for many.*

PERSONALLY SPEAKING *Ask God for more humility–whatever it costs, whatever it takes. But you're going to have to trust that He's heard and is answering, because you won't notice His humility in yourself.*

The whole foundation of prayer must be laid in humility, and the more a soul humbles itself in prayer, the more God lifts it up. The nearer we draw to God, the more this virtue should grow; if it does not, everything is lost. The most elegant prayer is unacceptable to God unless it is accompanied by humility.

You must think and understand Whom you are speaking to. In a thousand lifetimes we shall never manage to understand how our Lord deserves to be addressed; before His presence, even the angels tremble. It is well if you remember to Whom you are talking and who you are yourself, if only so that you may speak with proper reverence. For how will you be able to call the King "Your Highness," or to know what ceremonies are used in addressing a nobleman, if you do not properly understand what is His estate and what is your own?

Think about the certain kinds of humility which exist and of which I mean to speak. Some think it is humility not to believe that God is bestowing His gifts upon them. Let us clearly understand this: It is perfectly clear that God bestows His gifts without any merit whatever on our part. Let us be grateful to His Majesty for them. If we do not recognize the gifts received at His hands, we shall never be moved to love Him. It is a most certain truth that, the richer we see ourselves to be–confessing at the same time our poverty–the greater will be our progress and the more real will be our humility.

–Teresa of Avila

TERESA OF AVILA
(1515-1582)

She was one who proved through her life, influence, and writings that practical achievement and deep contemplation could find a peaceful home in the same person.

She entered a Spanish convent in 1533, but withdrew during a bout with serious illness. She would later reenter, but with a renewed purpose to live as a true servant of Christ. Known more for her mystical leanings (as expressed in *The Way of Perfection*), she also founded houses for nuns and friars and faithfully tended to the needs of the poor.

# CLOSED MINDED

"ANDY, YOU KNOW WHAT THAT STATE INVESTIGATOR'S GONNA GET FROM US WHEN HE GETS HERE?" "NO, BARN, WHAT?" "I'LL TELL YOU WHAT HE'S GONNA GET FROM US WHEN HE GETS HERE. THE BIG FREEZE." "WHAT?" "HE'S JUST INTERFERIN'. COMIN' DOWN HERE WHERE HE'S NOT WANTED. HE'S NOT GETTIN' ONE OUNCE OF OUR ATTENTION. I MEAN IT—YOU AND ME, ANGE. THE BIG FREEZE."

## James 1:13-15; Proverbs 4:20-27

*When tempted, no one should say, "God is tempting me." For God cannot be tempted by evil, nor does he tempt anyone; but each one is tempted when, by his own evil desire, he is dragged away and enticed. Then, after desire has conceived, it gives birth to sin; and sin, when it is full-grown, gives birth to death. . . .*

*My son, pay attention to what I say; listen closely to my words. Do not let them out of your sight, keep them within your heart; for they are life to those who find them and health to a man's whole body.*

*Above all else, guard your heart, for it is the wellspring of life. Put away perversity from your mouth; keep corrupt talk far from your lips.*

*Let your eyes look straight ahead, fix your gaze directly before you. Make level paths for your feet and take only ways that are firm.*

PERSONALLY SPEAKING *There's only one way to your heart, one door for Satan to try with his trickiest temptations. That door is your mind. And the knob's on your side. Don't turn it over to just anyone.*

Many men seek to overcome temptations only by fleeing from them, and they fall much more grievously into them. By only fleeing we may not overcome, but by patience and meekness we shall be stronger than our enemies. Thou shalt overcome them better little and little by patience and long-suffering with the help of God than with hardness and thine own importunity.

The beginning of all temptations is inconstancy of heart and little trust in God; for as a ship without governance is stirred hitherward and thitherward with the waves, so a man that is remiss and that holdeth not stedfastly his purpose is diversely tempted. Ofttimes, we know not what lieth in our power to do, but temptation openeth what we be.

Nevertheless, we ought to watch principally about the beginning, for then is the enemy soonest overcome if he be not suffered to enter unto the door of the mind; but anon, as he knocketh, meet him at entry. First, there cometh to mind a simple thought, after that a strong imagination, and then delectation and a shrewd moving–and assenting. So the wicked enemy, while he is not withstood in the beginning, entereth in little and little till he be all in; and the longer a man tarrieth in withstanding, the more feeble he waxeth continually and his enemy against him is more mighty.
–Thomas á Kempis

THOMAS Á
KEMPIS
(1380-1471)

He was from Germany, but departed for school in Holland at only thirteen. He was ordained as a priest in 1413 and spent his entire life in the priory of his older brother, John. He mainly worked as a copyist and is said to have transcribed the entire Bible four times. But his most famous writing by far is *The Imitation of Christ*, which was first issued anonymously in 1418 and attributed to various spiritual writers. It wasn't until 1441 that Thomas signed an extant copy, ascribing himself as the actual author.

# What's It All About?

The newsmagazines flash with the surprising details. Some Hollywood actor or well-known socialite has died overnight. The Internet gushes with tributes. The elite of the elite attend the memorial. They joke about how heaven will never be the same. And you wonder if amid all that hype, all that glamor, all that schmooze, they found what they were looking for.

## Ecclesiastes 12:1-4, 6-7, 13

Remember your Creator in the days of your youth, before the days of trouble come and the years approach when you will say, "I find no pleasure in them"–before the sun and the light and the moon and the stars grow dark, and the clouds return after the rain; when the keepers of the house tremble, and the strong men stoop, when the grinders cease because they are few, and those looking through the windows grow dim; when the doors to the street are closed and the sound of grinding fades; when men rise up at the sound of birds, but all their songs grow faint. . . .

Remember him–before the silver cord is severed, or the golden bowl is broken; before the pitcher is shattered at the spring, or the wheel broken at the well, and the dust returns to the ground it came from, and the spirit returns to God who gave it. . . .

Now all has been heard; here is the conclusion of the matter: Fear God and keep his commandments, for this is the whole duty of man.

PERSONALLY SPEAKING *There's a certain friend or family member who'll never admit to a serious thought until one day when life gets too deep for them to handle. Promise you'll be there when they're ready to talk.*

_____

_____

_____

_____

_____

_____

What is it for? What does it lead to? At first it seemed to me that these were aimless and irrelevant questions. The questions however began to repeat themselves frequently, and to demand replies more and more insistently. Then occurred what happens to everyone sickening with a mortal internal disease. At first trivial signs of indisposition appear to which the sick man pays no attention; then these signs reappear more and more often and merge into one uninterrupted period of suffering. The suffering increases, and before the sick man can look around, what he took for a mere indisposition has already become more important to him than anything else in the world!

That is what happened to me. I understood that if these questions constantly repeated themselves, they would have to be answered. And I tried to answer them. The questions seemed such stupid, simple, childish ones; but as soon as I touched them and tried to solve them I at once became convinced that they are not childish and stupid but the most important and profound of life's questions.

I would say to myself, "Very well; you will be more famous than Gogol or Pushkin or Shakespeare or Moliere, or than all the writers in the world—and what of it?" And I could find no reply at all. The questions would not wait, they had to be answered at once, and if I did not answer them it was impossible to live. I felt that what I had been standing on had collapsed and that I had nothing left under my feet. What I had lived on no longer existed, and there was nothing left.

–Leo Tolstoy

LEO TOLSTOY
(1828-1910)

Born in Russia to culture and prestige, he became one of her most notable novelists. *War and Peace* comes to mind. And *Anna Karenina*. But later in life, the rewards of success turned to "horror, loathing, and heart-rending pain" in his mind, and he accepted the Christian faith as his own, adopting a radical philosophy of nonresistance, rejection of the state, and disowning of his title and wealth. If nothing else, his later writings challenge the Christian to think deeply about the high cost of following Christ.

# BACK TO SCHOOL

THE TEACHERS YOU REALLY RESPECTED, THE ONES YOU LOOK BACK ON WITH A SMILING SENSE OF
ACCOMPLISHMENT, ARE THE ONES WHO PUSHED YOU BEYOND YOUR COMFORT ZONE, WHO SAW
SOMETHING IN YOU WORTH MOLDING AND SHAPING, WHO GREW IN YOU A LOVE FOR LEARNING
AND DISCOVERY. WOULD YOU EXPECT THE SPIRIT OF TRUTH, WHO TEACHES FROM THE VERY
HEART OF GOD, TO DELIVER ANY LESS?

## John 16:5-14

"Now I am going to him who sent me, yet none of you asks me,
'Where are you going?' Because I have said these things, you are filled
with grief.

"But I tell you the truth: It is for your good that I am going away.
Unless I go away, the Counselor will not come to you; but if I go, I
will send him to you.

"When he comes, he will convict the world of guilt in regard to
sin and righteousness and judgment: in regard to sin, because men
do not believe in me; in regard to righteousness, because I am going
to the Father, where you can see me no longer; and in regard to judgment, because the prince of this world now stands condemned.

"I have much more to say to you, more than you can now bear.
But when he, the Spirit of truth, comes, he will guide you into all
truth. He will not speak on his own; he will speak only what he
hears, and he will tell you what is yet to come. He will bring glory to
me by taking from what is mine and making it known to you."

PERSONALLY SPEAKING *Keep your paper out. Keep your pencil sharpened. Keep
your mind attentive and your assignments up to date. The Holy Spirit is talking,
teaching, instructing. And we've all got a lot to learn.*

_____

_____

_____

_____

_____

_____

# CLASSIC *Insights*

It is the privilege of each believer in Jesus Christ, even the humblest, to be "taught of God." This, of course, does not mean that we may not learn much from others who are taught of the Holy Spirit. If John had thought that, he would never have written his epistle to teach others. The man who is the most fully taught of God is the very one who will be most ready to listen to what God has taught others.

Much less does it mean that when we are taught of the Spirit, we are independent of the written Word of God, for the Word is the very place to which the Spirit, who is the Author of the Word, leads His pupils, and the instrument through which He instructs them.

But while we may learn much from men, we are not dependent upon them. We have a divine Teacher, the Holy Spirit. We shall never truly know the truth until we are thus taught directly by the Holy Spirit. No amount of mere human teaching, no matter who our teachers may be, will ever give us a correct and exact and full apprehension of the truth. Not even a diligent study of the Word either in English or in the original languages will give us a real understanding of the truth. We must be taught directly by the Holy Spirit. The one who is thus taught will understand the truth of God better, even if he does not know one word of Greek or Hebrew, than the one who knows Greek and Hebrew thoroughly, and all the cognate languages as well, but who is not taught of the Spirit.

–R. A. Torrey

R. A. TORREY
(1856-1928)

R. A. Torrey graduated from Yale, having studied some in Germany, and was ordained into the ministry in 1878. His long association with D. L. Moody resulted in his being named the first superintendent of the Moody Bible Institute, a post he held for nearly twenty years. He embarked on several world preaching tours during his life, serving also as dean of the Bible Institute of Los Angeles and pastor of the Church of the Open Door. He left behind numerous writings, including popular books on the work of the Holy Spirit.

# LASTING VALUE

THE POOR IN SPIRIT GET IT ALL. OH, THEY MISS OUT ON SOME THINGS. THEY MAY NOT COME TO WORK WITH THE FUNNY BITS FROM LAST NIGHT'S SITCOMS. THEY MAY NOT KNOW HOW MANY GAMES THE CUBS ARE OUT OF FIRST PLACE. THEY MAY NOT HAVE A CD PLAYER YET. BUT THEY'VE GOT SOMETHING WE COULD ALL USE A BIG SPOONFUL OF. PEACE OF MIND. TRUE CONTENTMENT. A STEADY WALK WITH GOD.

## 2 Corinthians 6:4-10; Luke 12:32-34

As servants of God we commend ourselves in every way: in great endurance; in troubles, hardships and distresses; in beatings, imprisonments and riots; in hard work, sleepless nights and hunger; in purity, understanding, patience and kindness; in the Holy Spirit and in sincere love; in truthful speech and in the power of God; with weapons of righteousness in the right hand and in the left; through glory and dishonor, bad report and good report; genuine, yet regarded as impostors; known, yet regarded as unknown; dying, and yet we live on; beaten, and yet not killed; sorrowful, yet always rejoicing; poor, yet making many rich; having nothing, and yet possessing everything. . . .

"Do not be afraid, little flock, for your Father has been pleased to give you the kingdom. Sell your possessions and give to the poor. Provide purses for yourselves that will not wear out, a treasure in heaven that will not be exhausted, where no thief comes near and no moth destroys. For where your treasure is, there your heart will be also."

PERSONALLY SPEAKING Is there too much going on in your life? Too many rooms that need painting, too many gutters that need cleaning, too many movies to choose from? Is this any way for a poor-in-spirit person to live?

The way to deeper knowledge of God is through the lonely valleys of soul poverty and abnegation of all things. The blessed ones who possess the Kingdom are they who have repudiated every external thing and have rooted from their hearts all sense of possessing.

These are the "poor in spirit." They have reached an inward state paralleling the outward circumstances of the common beggar in the streets of Jerusalem; that is what the word "poor" as Christ used it actually means. These blessed poor are no longer slaves to the tyranny of things. They have broken the yoke of the oppressor; and this they have done not by fighting but by surrendering. Though free from all sense of possessing, they yet possess all things. "Theirs is the kingdom of heaven."

Let me exhort you to take this seriously. It is not to be understood as mere Bible teaching to be stored away in the mind along with an inert mass of other doctrines. It is a marker on the road to greener pastures, a path chiseled against the steep sides of the mount of God. We dare not try to bypass it if we would follow on in this holy pursuit. We must ascend a step at a time. If we refuse one step we bring our progress to an end.

–A. W. Tozer

A. W. TOZER
(1897-1963)

One day when Tozer was a teenager, having moved from Pennsylvania to Akron, Ohio, the impassioned appeal of a street preacher caught his ear and pulled him from a non-Christian family into the family of God. Soon he was consumed with study and spiritual discovery—the pursuit that characterized his life's ministry, most of it invested as pastor of the Southside Alliance Church in Chicago. But his love of knowledge never outran his devotion to prayer. As one said, "He spent more time on his knees than at his desk."

# ACCEPT NO SUBSTITUTE

YOU CAN FIND A LOT OF SYNONYMS FOR LOVE IN THE LANGUAGE OF LIFE—A LOT OF THINGS
THAT SOUND AWFULLY RIGHT AND GOOD AND HOLY, A LOT OF WELL-REASONED PARAGRAPHS
AND POSITION PAPERS, A LOT OF DOING AND GOING AND SEEING AND BEING SEEN. BUT UNLESS
WE CAN SIGN IT WITH LOVE, WE HAVEN'T SAID ANYTHING TOO SPECIAL. WHEN WE OPEN UP
WITH LOVE, WE ALWAYS FIND THE RIGHT WORD TO SAY.

## 1 Corinthians 13:1-3, 8-10, 12-13

If I speak in the tongues of men and of angels, but have not love,
I am only a resounding gong or a clanging cymbal.

If I have the gift of prophecy and can fathom all mysteries and all
knowledge, and if I have a faith that can move mountains, but have
not love, I am nothing.

If I give all I possess to the poor and surrender my body to the
flames, but have not love, I gain nothing. . . .

Love never fails. But where there are prophecies, they will cease;
where there are tongues, they will be stilled; where there is knowledge, it will pass away. For we know in part and we prophesy in part,
but when perfection comes, the imperfect disappears. . . .

Now we see but a poor reflection as in a mirror; then we shall see
face to face. Now I know in part; then I shall know fully, even as I
am fully known.

And now these three remain: faith, hope and love. But the greatest of these is love.

PERSONALLY SPEAKING *The list on your day planner may be a mile long, and
the thoughts in your mind a mile a minute. Before you jump into something else,
ask God to help you soak everything you do or think in love.*

In the poem of Charity, we hear a music which has been beaten out in pain and effort upon the anvil of Paul's own heart. The high conviction which fills it, the lucid knowledge which it represents, had been won at the cost of many battles with arrogant intellect and dominant will.

One feels that Paul had at least considered, if he had not tried, the claims of all those kinds of spirituality which he here contrasts with the one all-conquering claim of Heavenly Love. Inspired utterance, prophetic genius, the abnormal powers which are often exhibited by selves which have attained to the illumined state we know that he possessed. He was naturally inclined to that deep brooding upon supernal mysteries which is so attractive to the speculative intellect. Practical altruism, untiring industry, high courage in bitter persecution, he had shown abundantly. One after another he reviews them. Prophet, ecstatic, philosopher, philanthropist, even martyr—every "way out" towards the Absolute which seems to the self-deluded human creature to be full of interest and promise, every type of deliberate spirituality—Paul tests and throws away. They are well enough in themselves, gifts which may indeed be "desired earnestly": he was no advocate of a pious stupidity, still less of a tame or indolent religion. But it is not by such means that Life makes her great saltatory ascents to freedom.

"A still more excellent way show I unto you."

–Evelyn Underhill

**EVELYN UNDERHILL (1875-1941)**

She was the only child of an aristocratic, but not deeply religious British family, educated in private schools and fully at ease with yachting and travel. But while visiting a Franciscan convent in 1907, she began a spiritual search that led to her professed conversion in 1911—and a lifetime love for Jesus Christ. She grew into one of the leading voices for Christian mysticism: an experiential, living union with the Lord that differs from mere magic in that it longs to give, not to get—to serve, not to be served.

# HAVE YOU NOTICED?

TO THE UNTRAINED EYE, IT'S JUST AN OLD MAN TOSSING BREAD CRUMBS TO THE DUCKS. BUT TO THE SPIRITUAL MIND, IT'S A LIVING PICTURE OF GOD'S TENDER CARE. TO THE UNOBSERVANT, IT'S JUST A BACKBREAKING JOB OF HOEING IN THE HOT SUN. TO THE INSIGHTFUL, IT'S A REMINDER TO KEEP THE WEEDS OF SIN FROM GETTING A FOOTHOLD. TO THE ONE WHOSE HEART IS ALWAYS SEEKING GOD, EVERYTHING SAYS SOMETHING.

## Psalm 139:1-7, 11-12, 14, 17-18

*O LORD, you have searched me and you know me. You know when I sit and when I rise; you perceive my thoughts from afar. You discern my going out and my lying down; you are familiar with all my ways. Before a word is on my tongue you know it completely, O LORD.*

*You hem me in–behind and before; you have laid your hand upon me. Such knowledge is too wonderful for me, too lofty for me to attain.*

*Where can I go from your Spirit? Where can I flee from your presence? . . . If I say, "Surely the darkness will hide me and the light become night around me," even the darkness will not be dark to you; the night will shine like the day, for darkness is as light to you. . . .*

*I praise you because I am fearfully and wonderfully made; your works are wonderful, I know that full well. . . . How precious to me are your thoughts, O God! How vast is the sum of them! Were I to count them, they would outnumber the grains of sand. When I awake, I am still with you.*

PERSONALLY SPEAKING *Be watchful through the day for little things–little lessons, little moments, little slivers of God's comfort and encouragement. He doesn't always talk where you can hear Him, unless you're listening.*

But it is time now, O my soul, to call your thoughts away from the multitudes of mankind, and to look carefully into yourself. Awake, awake to the work, O my heart! Enquire, examine, and take a strict account how your passionate powers are employed. Go over your various affections, and inquire of all of them: How stands your love to God?

Have you seen him, my soul, so as to love him? The love of the Creator will lead us to everlasting admiration. And if you love him, you will always find something new and wondrous in him, as your knowledge of him increases. Ask yourself, then, have you seen the glories and the graces of your God, so as to wonder at the infinite variety of his wisdom, the greatness of his majesty, and the condescensions of his mercy? Are his displays of glory in nature and providence, in the Bible and in the church, and especially in his beloved Son Jesus, the matter of your joyful meditation and high esteem? Does a sense of his transcendent grandeur and goodness strike you with a holy veneration, and with an awful delight? The love of so sublime and infinite a Being is naturally turned to pleasing adoration, and becomes an act of noble worship: Remember, O my soul, God alone must be adored.

–Isaac Watts

ISAAC WATTS
(1674-1748)

After becoming pastor of the London nonconformist church at Mark Lane in 1702, he never sought another post. But it is less for his preaching and much more for his hymns that he is best remembered. His music was first published in 1707, revealing a masterful gift for capturing the majesty of an all-powerful God and the epic story of man's redemption. Among his hymns still sung are "Jesus Shall Reign," "O God, Our Help in Ages Past," and "When I Survey the Wondrous Cross."

# REAL REPENTANCE

AS WE PRAY FOR OUR CHILDREN TO COME TO CHRIST, WE'RE ACTUALLY ASKING GOD TO SHOWER ON THEM THE SORROW OF REPENTANCE, THE STAB OF SHAME, THE PIERCING PAIN OF CONVICTION. WE'RE ASKING HIM TO BRING THEIR SINS INTO FULL VIEW AT WHATEVER COST IS REQUIRED, SO THAT IN THE DEATH EXPERIENCE OF REPENTANCE, THEY'LL FIND THE REFRESHING LIFE OF JESUS CHRIST. THERE'S NO OTHER WAY.

## 2 Corinthians 7:8–13a

*Even if I caused you sorrow by my letter, I do not regret it. Though I did regret it—I see that my letter hurt you, but only for a little while—yet now I am happy, not because you were made sorry, but because your sorrow led you to repentance. For you became sorrowful as God intended and so were not harmed in any way by us.*

*Godly sorrow brings repentance that leads to salvation and leaves no regret, but worldly sorrow brings death.*

*See what this godly sorrow has produced in you: what earnestness, what eagerness to clear yourselves, what indignation, what alarm, what longing, what concern, what readiness to see justice done. At every point you have proved yourselves to be innocent in this matter.*

*So even though I wrote to you, it was not on account of the one who did the wrong or of the injured party, but rather that before God you could see for yourselves how devoted to us you are. By all this we are encouraged.*

PERSONALLY SPEAKING *Repentance requires eating the boiled okra and brussel sprouts of your sin. But in tasting how bitter your transgressions really are, you'll find them changed into the sweet flavor of forgiveness.*

Repentance permanent and deep to thy poor suppliant give,
Indulge me at thy feet to weep, When thou hast bid me live;
When thou record'st my sins no more, O may I still lament,
A sinner, saved by grace adore, A pardon'd penitent.

Thou will'st thy followers to request fullness of joy in thee,
To covet gifts the chief, the best; But grief seems best for me:
My sins I never can forget, Even when thy face appears,
Or covet but to kiss thy feet, And wash them with my tears.

I ask no aught whereof to boast, But let
   me feel applied
The blood that ransomed sinners lost,
   And by thy cross abide;
Myself the chief of sinners know, Till all
   my griefs are passed,
And of my gracious acts below,
   Repentance be the last.

–Charles Wesley

**CHARLES WESLEY**
(1707-1788)

He was the eighteenth of Samuel and Susanna Wesley's nineteen children, this sweet singer of the Methodist movement. And when Christ fully arrested his heart in 1738, he poured himself into the evangelistic ministry in England, preaching in open-air settings, visiting prisons, telling everyone who'd listen to him about the Lord Jesus Christ. Yet beyond his speaking successes, he is perhaps most noted as the composer of more than seven thousand sacred hymns, many of which continue to bless today's church.

_____

_____

_____

_____

_____

_____

# UNITED WE STAND

IF YOU DON'T PROMISE YOURSELF THAT YOU'RE NOT GOING TO TALK BEHIND SOMEONE'S BACK, IF YOU DON'T REMEMBER TO PRAY FOR THE ONE WHO STRIKES YOU AS SO OBNOXIOUS, YOU'LL FORGET IN THE HEAT OF THE DAY TO LET YOUR COOLER, MORE CHRISTIAN HEAD PREVAIL. AND YOU'LL BE SORRY AGAIN FOR THE THINGS YOU THOUGHT OR SAID. GOD SEES THE PART THAT'S EVEN WORSE THAN YOU SEE . . . AND STILL LOVES.

## Romans 12:10-18; Matthew 7:1-2

*Be devoted to one another in brotherly love. Honor one another above yourselves. Never be lacking in zeal, but keep your spiritual fervor, serving the Lord.*

*Be joyful in hope, patient in affliction, faithful in prayer. Share with God's people who are in need. Practice hospitality.*

*Bless those who persecute you; bless and do not curse. Rejoice with those who rejoice; mourn with those who mourn.*

*Live in harmony with one another. Do not be proud, but be willing to associate with people of low position. Do not be conceited.*

*Do not repay anyone evil for evil. Be careful to do what is right in the eyes of everybody. If it is possible, as far as it depends on you, live at peace with everyone. . . .*

*Do not judge, or you too will be judged. For in the same way you judge others, you will be judged, and with the measure you use, it will be measured to you.*

PERSONALLY SPEAKING *Imagine that you're sitting at the lunch table with some person you dislike—just him and you. How would you treat him differently than you do in a crowd? Or when he's not looking?*

In the name, then, and in the strength of God, let us resolve, first, not to hurt one another; to do nothing unkind or unfriendly to each other, nothing which we would not have done to ourselves. Rather, let us endeavor after every instance of a kind, friendly, and Christian behavior toward each other.

Let us resolve, secondly, God being our helper, to speak nothing harsh or unkind of each other. The sure way to avoid this is to say all the good we can both of and to one another. . . .

Let us, thirdly, resolve to harbor no unkind thought, no unfriendly temper toward each other. Let us lay the ax to the root of the tree; let us examine all that rises in our heart, and suffer no disposition there which is contrary to tender affection. Then shall we easily refrain from unkind actions and words when the very root of bitterness is cut up.

Let us, fourthly, endeavor to help each other on in whatever way we are agreed leads to the kingdom. So far as we can, let us always rejoice to strengthen each other's hands in God. Above all, let us each take heed to himself (since each must give an account of himself to God) that he fall not short of the religion of love; that he be not condemned in that he himself approveth.

–John Wesley

JOHN WESLEY
(1703-1791)

Even after a missions undertaking to the United States with his brother Charles in 1735, he found himself in need of true salvation and gave his heart to Christ in 1738. Back in England, he set out "to reform the nation, particularly the Church, and to spread Scriptural holiness over the land." This he did through widespread open-air preaching, tireless travels to the hamlets of the common man, and the establishing of organizations and societies that resulted in the Methodist manner of missions and church government.

# HELD ACCOUNTABLE

IT'S GOOD TO SEE ACCOUNTABILITY COMING BACK IN STYLE. IT'S GREAT TO SEE MEN AND WOMEN GETTING TOGETHER TO TALK AND TO SHARE, TO CONFESS THEIR SINS AND TO CELEBRATE THEIR SUCCESSES, AND TO ENJOY THE TOUGH-NOSED BLESSING OF HAVING SOMEONE TO CALL YOU ON EVERY BLUFF. THE MORE WE OPEN OUR LIVES FOR CLOSER EXAMINATION, THE MORE WE BECOME IN PRIVATE WHAT WE PROFESS TO BE IN PUBLIC.

## Psalm 141:5; Proverbs 9:9; Ecclesiastes 4:9-12; Psalm 94:12-14

*Let a righteous man strike me–it is a kindness; let him rebuke me–it is oil on my head. My head will not refuse it. Yet my prayer is ever against the deeds of evildoers. . . .*

*Instruct a wise man and he will be wiser still; teach a righteous man and he will add to his learning. . . .*

*Two are better than one, because they have a good return for their work: If one falls down, his friend can help him up. But pity the man who falls and has no one to help him up!*

*Also, if two lie down together, they will keep warm. But how can one keep warm alone? Though one may be overpowered, two can defend themselves. A cord of three strands is not quickly broken. . . .*

*Blessed is the man you discipline, O LORD, the man you teach from your law; you grant him relief from days of trouble, till a pit is dug for the wicked. For the LORD will not reject his people; he will never forsake his inheritance.*

PERSONALLY SPEAKING *Have you found a small group of caring, Christian friends you can open your heart to? Be willing to be vulnerable enough to reveal who you are and loving enough to invest your life in another.*

_____

_____

_____

_____

_____

_____

As man in his present condition cannot always stand upright, but by reason of the frailty of his nature cannot but fall; one eminent reason why two are better than one, or, in other words, one great advantage of religious society is, "That when they fall, the one will lift up his fellow." And an excellent reason this, indeed! For alas! When we reflect how prone we are to be drawn into error in our judgments, and into vice in our practice; and how unable, at least how very unwilling, to espy or correct our own miscarriages; when we consider how apt the world is to flatter us in our faults, and how few there are so kind as to tell us the truth; what an inestimable privilege must it be to have a set of true, judicious, hearty friends about us, continually watching over our souls, to inform us where we have fallen, and to warn us that we fall not again for the future. Surely it is such a privilege, that (to use the words of an eminent Christian) we shall never know the value thereof, till we come to glory.

But this is not all; for supposing that we could always stand upright, yet whosoever reflects on the difficulties of religion in general, and his own propensity to lukewarmness and indifference in particular, will find that he must be zealous as well as steady, if ever he expects to enter the kingdom of heaven. Here, then, the wise man points out to us another excellent reason why two are better than one. "Again, if two lie together, then they have heat; but how can one be warm alone?"

–George Whitefield

GEORGE WHITEFIELD (1714-1770)

He began his fiery preaching career with a bang—blistering the ears of his homefolk in Gloucester so soundly, a complaint was made to the bishop that he had driven fifteen people mad. But after restraining himself to the pulpit for a short while, he joined forces with the Wesleys and began a lifelong ministry of open-air preaching, regularly delivering up to twenty of his trademark, impassioned revival messages a week, traveling many times to Scotland and the United States, where he died shortly after giving his last sermon.

# MODEL CITIZENS

IF THERE'S ANY DEBATE ABOUT HOW MUCH OF AN IMPACT PRAYER HAS ON A NATION, IF THERE'S ANY QUESTION ABOUT THE ROLE GOD PLAYS IN DIRECTING ITS LEADERS, IF THERE'S ANY WONDER WE'VE FOUND OURSELVES IN THE SHAPE THAT WE'RE IN, LET'S QUIT TALKING AND START PRAYING. LET'S QUIT POINTING FINGERS AND START REPENTING. LET'S WEEP UNTIL THE WINDS OF REVIVAL BLOW. THEN THEY'LL KNOW.

## Psalm 33:12-22

Blessed is the nation whose God is the LORD, the people he chose for his inheritance.

From heaven the LORD looks down and sees all mankind; from his dwelling place he watches all who live on earth–he who forms the hearts of all, who considers everything they do.

No king is saved by the size of his army; no warrior escapes by his great strength. A horse is a vain hope for deliverance; despite all its great strength it cannot save.

But the eyes of the LORD are on those who fear him, on those whose hope is in his unfailing love, to deliver them from death and keep them alive in famine.

We wait in hope for the LORD; he is our help and our shield. In him our hearts rejoice, for we trust in his holy name. May your unfailing love rest upon us, O LORD, even as we put our hope in you.

PERSONALLY SPEAKING *Your prayers can make a difference. The intercession of God's people and the response of God's church can bring revival to this land. Millions are waiting for a touch from God–and a word from you.*

Let true Christians, with becoming earnestness, strive in all things to recommend their profession and to put to silence the vain scorn of ignorant objections. Let them boldly assert the cause of Christ in an age when so many who bear the name of Christian are ashamed of Him. Let them accept the duty to serve, if not actually to save, their country. Let them serve not by political interference, but by that sure and radical benefit of restoring the influence of true religion and of raising the standard of morality.

Let them pray continually for their country at this time of national difficulty. We bear the marks only too plainly of a declining empire. Who can say how intercession before the Governor of the universe may avert for a while our ruin. It may appear before the eyes of the world foolishness for real Christians so to pray, yet we believe from Scripture that God will be disposed to favor the nation to which His servants belong.

Boldly I must confess that I believe the national difficulties we face result from the decline of religion and morality among us. I must confess equally boldly that my own solid hopes for the well-being of my country depend, not so much on her navies and armies, nor on the wisdom of her rulers, nor on the spirit of her people, as on the persuasion that she still contains many who love and obey the Gospel of Christ. I believe that their prayers may yet prevail.

–William Wilberforce

WILLIAM
WILBERFORCE
(1759-1833)

Hustled off as a boy to boarding school to avert his religious leanings, he wasn't truly confronted with the gospel until traveling at age twenty-five with a local clergyman, being converted as they read the Scriptures together. He embarked on a career in the British Parliament, most notably as England's tireless voice for anti-slavery legislation. Every year for eighteen years, he brought his bill to the House of Commons until it was finally adopted in 1806, though not fully implemented until one year before his death.

# Credits

**Anselm** *St. Anselm's Book of Meditations and Prayers*

**Aquinas** *Summa Theologica*

**Augustine** *The Confessions*

**Bacon** *The Essays of Francis Bacon*

**Baillie** *A Diary of Private Prayer* (Charles Scribner's Sons, 1949). Copyright renewed 1977 by Ian Fowler Baillie. Reprinted with the permission of Scribner, a division of Simon & Schuster.

**Barth** *God Here and Now* (Harper & Row, 1964). Copyright by Theologischer Verlag Zurich. Used by permission.

**Baxter** *The Saints' Everlasting Rest*

**Bernard** *On Loving God*

**Bonar** *God's Way of Peace*

**Bonhoeffer** *The Cost of Discipleship* (SCM Press Ltd., 1959)

**Booth** *Aggressive Christianity* (World Wide Publications, 1993)

**Bounds** *The Necessity of Prayer*

**Brainerd** *The Life and Diary of David Brainerd*

**Brengle** *The Soul Winner's Secret*

**Bullinger** *Zwingli and Bullinger,* translated by G.W. Bromiley, from the Library of Christian Classics (Westminster John Knox Press, 1953). Used by permission.

**Bunyan** *A Holy Life*

**Bushnell** *Sermons on Christ and His Salvation*

**Calvin** *Institutes of the Christian Religion*

**Carmichael** *Rose from Brier* (Christian Literature Crusade) Used by permission.

**Caussade** *The Sacrament of the Present Moment* (Harper Collins, 1982)

**Chambers** *My Utmost for His Highest*

**Chapman** *Present Day Parables*

**Chaucer** *Canterbury Tales in Contemporary Verse* (Franklin Library, 1974)

**Chesterton** *Orthodoxy*

**Chrysostom** *Baptismal Instructions* (Longmans Green & Co., 1963)

**Clarke** *Clavis Biblica*

**Clement** *Epistle to the Corinthians*

**Cyprian** *On the Advantage of Patience*

**Dagg** *Manual of Theology*

**Dale** *Christian Doctrine*

**Denney** *The Death of Christ*

**Donne** *Devotions upon Emergent Occasions*

**Edwards** *Resolutions*

**Erasmus** *Enchiridion Militis Christian: An English Version* (Oxford University Press, 1981). Used by permission of The Council of the Early English Text Society

**Finney** *Sermons on Gospel Themes*

**Flavel** *Keeping the Heart*

**Foster** *Celebration of Discipline* (Harper San Francisco, 1988)

**Francis of Assisi** *The Little Flowers of St. Francis*

**Francis de Sales** *Introduction to a Devout Life*

**Gore** *The Incarnation of the Son of God*

**Graham** *Hope for the Troubled Heart* (Word Publishing, 1993). Used by permission. All rights reserved.

**Guthrie** *The Christian's Great Interest*

**Havner** Unknown source

**Henry** *Moments of Meditation with Matthew Henry*

**Hurnard** *Hinds' Feet on High Places* (Tyndale House Publishers, 1975). Used by permission. All rights reserved.

**Jones** *The Trail of Life in the Middle Years*

**Jowett** *Sharing His Suffering*

**Justin** *The Second Apology of Justin*

**Kierkegaard** *Works of Love*

**King** *Loving Your Enemies*

**Knox** *A Declaration of the True Nature and Object of Prayer*

**Law** *A Serious Call to a Devout and Holy Life*

**Lewis** *The Problem of Pain* (Macmillan, 1962)

**Liguori** *Uniformity with God's Will*

**Luther** *Christian Liberty*

**MacDonald** *Unspoken Sermons*

**Menno** *The Complete Writings of Menno Simons*

**Meyer** "God Is Near" *Great Pulpit Masters, Volume VI* (Revell, 1950). Used by permission.

**Milton** *Paradise Lost*

**Moody** *The Overcoming Life*

**Muggeridge** *Confessions of a Twentieth Century Pilgrim* (Harper & Row, 1988)

**Murray** *The True Vine*

**Nee** *The Spiritual Man* (Christian Fellowship Publishers, 1968). Used by permission.

**Neibuhr, Reinhold** "Love and Law" (Christian Century Foundation, 1956). Used by permission from the January 1956 issue of *The Christian Ministry.*

**Niebuhr, Richard** *Christ and Culture* (Harper & Row, 1951)

**Owen** *Of Communion with God*

**Packer** *Knowing God* (InterVarsity Press, 1973). Used by permission.

**Pascal** *Mind on Fire* (Bethany House, 1997). Used by permission.

**Patrick** *The Confession*

**Sayers** "The Greatest Drama Ever Staged" *Creed and Chaos.* Reprinted by permission of the Estate of Dorothy L. Sayers and the Watkins/Loomis Agency.

**Schaeffer** *True Spirituality* (Tyndale House Publishers, 1971) Used by permission. All rights reserved.

**Sheldon** *In His Steps*

**Singh** *At the Master's Feet*

**Smith** *A Christian's Secret of a Happy Life*

**South** *Upon the Resurrection*

**Spurgeon** *Sermons*

**Tauler** "Sermon for St. Peter's Day" *The History and Life of the Reverend Doctor John Tauler*

**Taylor, Hudson** *A Ribbon of Blue and Other Stories*

**Taylor, Jeremy** *The Rules and Exercises of Holy Living*

**Teresa** *A Life of Prayer* (Multnomah, 1983)

**Thomas** *The Imitation of Christ*

**Tolstoy** *A Confession*

**Torrey** *The Person and Work of the Holy Spirit*

**Tozer** *The Pursuit of God*

**Underhill** *The Mystic Way*

**Watts** *Divine Love Is the Commanding Passion*

**Wesley, Charles** *Charles Wesley: Evangelist & Poet*

**Wesley, John** *Letter to a Roman Catholic*

**Whitefield** "The Necessity and Benefits of a Religious Society" *Select Sermons of George Whitefield*

**Wilberforce** *Real Christianity*

# Scripture References Used

# Scripture References Used

# Scripture References Used

# Notes

# Notes

# Notes

# Notes

# Notes

# Notes